Envision Lead Grow

Releasing
The Boss Within

—————————

Dr Angela D Reddix

Envision Lead Grow – Releasing the Boss Within
Copyright © 2020 by ELG Management Group

ELG Management Group
1215 North Military Highway
Suite 210
Norfolk, VA 23502
United States
ISBN 978-0-578-40580-3

Library of Congress Control Number 2020901046

Printed in USA

Back Cover Photo Credit Brian Waldron Photography

Dedication

My grandmother, Olivia Maggie Dyson, I feel your hand gently guiding me every day.

My mother for being courageous enough to be the first.

My extended family who shaped my experience along the way.

My circle of incredible women, who cheer me to and through every challenge.

Every ARDX Associate who entered the enterprise, I learned from every experience.

My Envision Lead Grow family, Core Team, mentors, parents, partners, and my beloved ELG Girl Bosses.

My A- Team, Anyssa, Ahmon, and Ayla. You make me a better woman.

My forever boyfriend, Pete. Look what we have created, together.

Table of Contents

Chapter One

Little Girls Who Dream

MY BLISS AS A CHILD began when I arrived home from school. I curled up on our brown shag carpet and gently placed the needle on the vinyl to listen to Minnie Ripperton's "Lovin' You." Her voice was soothing and cleared away the doldrums of my life while I waited for my mother to come home. I loved to hear the crackle of the needle as it played through the imperfections of the record, while I lay on the floor with the album cover and read along with the lyrics.

Then I'd switch to Michael Jackson so I could try out some of my dance moves to his album *Off the Wall*. I never felt alone as long as the old familiar voices were there to keep me company.

I didn't want to tell my mother how lonely I

felt as a child. She was a single mom and I didn't want to burden her. I only wanted to make her proud of me and lighten her load whenever I could. I didn't want to disturb her life with my trivial feelings, and so I smiled, and I sang to my favorite records.

The times I wanted a sweet lullaby, I played what would become the soundtrack of my life. Deniece Williams belted:

Black Butterfly
Set the skies on fire
Rise up even higher
So the ageless winds of time can catch your wings...

I had no idea at the time how impactful that song would be. I was just this young teenage girl, taken away from the only real family I had known in Norfolk, Virginia, and thrust into a community in Virginia Beach, Virginia, where no one looked like me. I felt so alone.

In many cultures, black butterflies are considered bad omens. If a black butterfly is the first butterfly seen in the spring, it is a portent of terrible storms and weather.

But listening to Williams sing:

Morning light
Silken dream to flight
As the darkness gave way to dawn
You've survived
Now your moment has arrived
Now your dream has finally been born...

It didn't seem like something negative. It was something beautiful, filled with hope for the future.

Some believe that the black butterfly represents death and rebirth. When caterpillars transform into cocoons, they leave their old identity behind. They wait in a constricted state for the day they will emerge anew. When they finally break free of their self-constructed enclosure and dry their new wings, they emerge as something new. Something wonderful, ready to fly into the sky and soar to new heights.

'Cause now that you're free
And the world has come to see
Just how proud and beautiful you are...

Humble Beginnings

My mother was living her dream. She had started as a caterpillar. One of ten kids living in the projects in Norfolk, Virginia, in an area called Liberty Park. There was little hope she would ever break free of the bonds that often shackle those in poverty. She was the second child, but from an early age, she had a glow about her. She was destined for a different path from the family around her and those who walked before her.

It was the late 1960s, and segregation was still very much alive in the South. She went to Booker T. Washington High School because that is where all African-Americans had to go. She was brilliant, and she accelerated past her peers. She skipped two grades and graduated at the young age of sixteen as her school's valedictorian.

What happened next made her a hometown hero in my book. She was offered a full scholarship to the University of Pennsylvania as a math major. My mother was breaking all the records, and my grandmother made sure she was able to get out of Norfolk and make something of herself.

Back in those days, my family didn't have a

car, and so my mother stepped onto the Greyhound bus, with a bag and some sandwiches, and was off to make a life for herself. When she arrived, there were not many people who looked like her, but she had this determination to succeed.

May 1968 was the end of my mother's first year in college and also the year I was born. My mother had become pregnant, and the timing of my birth could not have been more perfect because she could not miss any school. She was on a full scholarship and could not miss a day. I cannot imagine what it must have been like for her—a teenager, pregnant, far away from home for the first time, and trying to make it at an Ivy League school. I was born the same year Dr. Martin Luther King Jr. was assassinated. It was a dark time in American history, and the future was unsure. My mother had one shot at making it work, and she didn't want to give up on her dream.

Sometimes fulfilled dreams come with sacrifice. My grandmother agreed to take me as one of her own and raise me so that my mother could finish school. I grew up with aunts and uncles who were more like siblings.

After my mom graduated with her bachelor's

degree, she decided to go to NYU School of Law, which was even further away. This meant she could only visit me during holidays, summers, and occasionally on weekends. My grandmother treated me like her own child and distance would not allow me to have a strong relationship with my mother. My grandmother was my world. But even with all her love, I could still feel a void in my life. Other children at school and in the neighborhood had moms and some had dads present in their life, and while technically I had a mom, I hardly knew her. As a child, she was this strange woman who appeared and vanished quickly.

I'm sure she loved me, and I'm sure that she wanted to make a better life for us. While my mother was finishing her degree, my grandmother moved from a small unit in the projects to a single-family home in Park Place community. It was still in a lower-income part of town, but to me, it was a huge step up. It is where I learned to ride my bike. I remember all the neighborhood children would come by and play. And our front porch was the neighbor party place. We had holidays full of joy and love in that house. It was home to me.

Once my mother finished school, she was

offered a job in downtown Norfolk. I moved into her apartment, but I was still close to my grandmother's home. As my mother moved up the corporate ladder, so did our living arrangements, which eventually landed us in Virginia Beach, Virginia, where everything changed. I had barely any time to mourn my former life when I found myself in the fifth grade, in a new town, where few if any of the people looked like me. I was already struggling as all girls do at that age to establish my identity. My body was changing, my hormones were raging, and now I had been taken from my life, my family, my neighborhood, to live with a woman I had just begun to know, in a community of predominantly white upper-class families, where I knew no one.

I loved my mother, and I was not angry at her. I wanted to be the perfect child, and so I held my feelings of isolation inside during middle school and into high school. I wanted to please my mother and so I was an overachiever in school.

It was just mom and me. When I was younger, I had a babysitter, who like everyone else didn't look like me. As I grew older, I became a latchkey kid, coming home every day after school, often feeding myself, getting my homework done, cleaning the house, and waiting for my mother to return home.

I had no one to relate to, and I felt stifled and suffocated much the same way I believe a caterpillar must feel while it is in its cocoon. There was no room. No air. No freedom. It seemed very dark and hopeless.

I tried clubs at school to connect with other kids my age. I was on the student council and even in the Latin club. I had friends, but I still didn't know who I was. I missed my family in Norfolk. I missed my grandmother. I missed my home.

I don't believe my mother ever really understood how I felt. She was what I call a provider. She made sure I had everything I ever needed physically. I had beautiful clothes, good food, and a charming place to live. My grandmother, on the other hand, was a nurturer. While she could not provide me more than the minimum basic needs, she nurtured and fed my soul.

My mother was a woman of numbers and practicality. She was this young woman in her twenties with a degree, a good job, and a child.

I believe she felt some of the loneliness and isolation I did, but it was never something she talked about. She was a hero. She had made it out of the projects and had a good life. She was the first in the family to leave her hometown. The first to go to an Ivy League school and graduate. She was the first to own a car. She had no right to complain because she had everything she could want. I felt much the same way. Compared to my old life, I was living like royalty, so how could I be so miserable inside? I didn't really appreciate how my mom might have felt until I had achieved my own success in my business, and I felt isolated. I didn't have anyone that I could talk to or relate to. I believe my mother felt much the same way.

But I did connect with her one way, and that was through music. My mother loved all kinds of music and would bring home records of her favorite artists to share and sing to. It was my way of finding a little warmth in the cold existence of my life. So even when she was working long hours, I could spread all the records around me, read the lyrics and sing along, and for those moments, I didn't feel so alone.

I wonder, do caterpillars dream while they lay

tightly wound in their shroud? Do they fantasize about breaking free and flying? Do they imagine the heights they can reach?

Most little girls dream of who they will be when they grow up. I had two role models—the nurturer and the provider. I wanted to be both of them. I wanted to be like my grandmother: loving, supportive, and with an octopus-like ability to wrap her arms around many people at once. She had an impeccable sixth sense to understand the unique needs of her children and grandchildren without them speaking a word to her.

I wanted to be a provider like my mother: successful, practical, and driven. She was always disciplined with money. She didn't believe in getting into debt. Whatever credit you might use, you pay it back immediately.

I have a good relationship with money today because of her. She built her own townhome. She paid for all the furniture with cash. She had high standards, and all the things she owned were of high quality. It was always about *quality* rather than *quantity*.

She paid for my college with cash. I didn't have loans and didn't have to worry about finances.

I could just concentrate on my studies. She showed me how she did it. I remember we ate nothing but spinach for two months. Spinach soup, spinach salad, spinach everything. Back then, spinach was really cheap. She had set a goal of saving money. The money she was saving from groceries, she put in a jar. I could see the money growing every week. That was such a powerful lesson for me.

She was a provider, and my 14-year-old self didn't understand what powerful lessons she was giving me at the time. It was not until years later when I was on my own that I realized the gift she had given me. Those financial lessons and goal setting have served me in all aspects of my life. Even though I was experiencing isolation and a crisis of identity in those formative years, when I emerged, I was so much more prepared than I could have imagined.

College: My Emergence from the Cocoon

I struggled so much with my identity during my early years, I was glad to have the opportunity to move somewhere new and hopefully find that piece missing from my life. My life purpose and sense of belonging.

One of my dreams as a child was to become a teacher. I had a lot of time alone at home, and so one of the games I played was school. I would line up my dolls and give them lessons. One of my best students was my Rodney Allen Rippy doll (he was a child star at the time).

In high school, I toyed with the idea of majoring in education, but my mother didn't want me to pursue that path. She didn't believe that becoming a teacher was much of a return on her educational investment in me, and so I couched the idea.

Thankfully, I found the place and the people I needed. In college, I found my first tribe. From the moment my feet touched the mountains around James Madison University, I knew I had found the place I had been looking for all my life. I discovered people who were like me. They shared the same ideas, values, and hunger to make an impact in the world. We forged what would become lifelong relationships. These women are now the godmothers and aunties to my child. I met my husband while attending. The community ignited my passion and helped me build a stronger concept of who I was and what I was meant to do in the world.

I felt appreciated for my work ethic, my processes, and my values. I became involved in groups around campus and took leadership roles. I was that butterfly emerging from my long dark journey in the cocoon. I was beginning to spread my wings. I was preparing to soar.

I graduated with a business marketing degree. It was the beginning of becoming who I am today. I accomplished what I had sought for many years to do: I made my mother proud of me. I graduated from college and landed a highly coveted and lucrative job as a pharmaceutical sales rep. My wings were ready to help me soar. Everything was in place and my success assured.

If you are at the top of a ten-story building, looking down, you have the sense of being high up and that you are on the top of everything. You made it to the pinnacle. That perspective is dwarfed by those looking down from the top of a mountain. The ten-story building looks small and toy-like. I was flying high and beating my wings, but I was not quite soaring yet.

The job for me was simple. I watched my favorite soap operas during the day, and then I went to the dentist's offices before they closed and was very successful in sales. The problem was it was too easy for me. It was not challenging enough. I knew I could do much more in my heart of hearts. I was destined to soar higher.

I met with my district director and handed him my resignation. I had a company car, an expense account, benefits, good pay, and freedom, so why did I give it up? I could not stay in the position and be true to my heart and to my passion. I needed a challenge.

I had a sizable savings account. Even though I was living at home, I paid rent to my mother, but I didn't have many other expenses. I decided to pack up all my belongings and I moved to Washington, D.C., without a job. I was ready for my next adventure.

I moved in with my paternal aunt, uncle, and cousins for a time. This was a comfortable place to start my new life. Growing up, I spent every summer with them. I was filled with such found memories. This was a safe place to land. I started in the telecommunications field and quickly rose up the ranks within a telecom company. It is interesting that as we grow into adulthood, we say we are going to be different from our parents. That in some way, we are going to forge a new path. In my case, I did create an original path, but it started much as my mother's did, as she too she enjoyed her career in the telecommunications industry.

Transforming Dreams into Reality

When we set goals for ourselves, it is remarkable how we achieve them. We set our intention, and the universe moves to accommodate our wishes. This is not a quick-wish scheme. We cannot just dream it and wait for the doorbell to ring with someone holding a check. I was not raised with any sense of entitlement. My mother made sure of that. From the time I was a teenager, I had a job and worked for the things I wanted.

My belief is that faith without work is dead. Once we put our intentions out into the world, it is time to put on our power heels and begin the work.

When I arrived in D.C., there was a building

that caught my eye in Greenbelt, Maryland. I loved the way the building looked, and I made a promise to myself that I would work in that building one day. Every day on my way to my new job, I saw that same building and thought about what it would be like to be there someday.

Eventually, I began working for CDSC a Bell Atlantic company (now Verizon). Yep, you guessed it. I started working in that building that I dreamed about working in for years.

Since I was going to start in sales, I was sent to a six-week training class. I walked into class and saw these well-dressed, immaculately groomed people. I again made a promise to myself: I wanted to be one of those people. It turned out that they were our trainers. I realized that I could be a teacher in the corporate world, and I knew that was what I wanted to do. I could fulfill the dream that I had as a teenager of being an educator. What I realized then is that sometimes God answers our prayers, but they are not always in the way we perceived it happening or in our concept of timing.

The Tin Woman

Some of our most excellent mentors come to us at times we don't always expect. We don't always immediately understand their impact on our lives until later.

In the story *The Wizard of Oz*, Dorothy hurts her head during a storm and is transported into the wondrous land of Oz. She meets different characters like the Lion, the Scarecrow, and the Tin Man. Each of those characters becomes an essential person in her journey. By meeting each of them, she realizes something is missing from their lives, and because of that missing part, they are often misunderstood.

The scarecrow lacks a brain but wants to be seen as smart. The lion lacks courage and often runs away because he is scared. The tin man lacks a heart. Dorothy accepts each of these people into her journey with a promise she will help them when they reach the all-powerful Wizard of Oz.

When they reach the wizard, they realize he is nothing but a man. A man with influence and creativity. He explains to each of them that they already had the parts of themselves that they were seeking, locked within. Dorothy, through her understanding, acceptance, and love, had helped each of them find their lost parts.

When I was assigned my first unit to work in, I met my tin woman. Everyone said she was heartless and harsh. People were afraid of her and didn't want to work with her. I decided to be like Dorothy and open my heart to her.

I could sense the pain in her and in the team. I was a girl of 23, but I felt I could help her. I made a deal with her to trust me, and I would rally the team together and heal the wounds there. I would get everyone on the same page working together. I spoke to the team and explained that she was under pressure from leadership to produce, but that we all needed to work together, and they did. I created a friend and ally.

She gave me the greatest gift in return: wisdom and feedback. I was this young girl who liked to wear cute little dresses to work. She pulled me into her office and told me that if I really wanted to succeed and work my way up, I needed to dress more professionally. She told me this because she genuinely wanted me to succeed, not to put me down. If she didn't care, she would have remained silent only to watch me fail and become frustrated. That left an impression on me and shaped my management style for years to come.

I told her of my desire to become a trainer. She advised me to go back to school to get my master's degree in training and development. I went to Bowie State University, which was only fifteen minutes from the office. Because I had developed an ally, she advocated for me. I finished the program in two years. She supported me the whole time, even allowing me to adjust my work schedule to accommodate my class schedule. The company paid for my tuition.

I helped her solve her pain, and she helped me solve mine. I was able to bring someone into my vision and in turn, I was in hers. The week after I graduated, I transitioned into my new position as a trainer. I remember the feeling the first day I walked into the training room. I felt powerful and alive. I had become one of those people I met a few years prior and had been so impressed with. I had manifested my dream to be a teacher, and now I had a roomful of students looking up to me. None of them ever topped my favorite student, Rodney Allen Rippy.

My work as a trainer and my college education presented a new opportunity in another company. I was offered a job as a training project manager for Visa International in a beautiful building in Northern Virginia. I had a corner glass office and an excellent 401K match; for every dollar I put in, the company matched with four dollars. I had a terrific benefits package, my manager was very supportive, and I had a great rapport with her. It seemed I had everything I wanted, until one day when I received a phone call from Rozita, a woman who remembered me from graduate school.

"I remembered how you carried yourself in school and your presentations. I have started my own business, and we have our first big contract with Kaiser Permanente," she said. "I have to roll out a project with national implementation and I need your help." She had called the school to get my information and wanted me to go to all the sites to help set up the project as a program director.

I knew nothing about healthcare, and I didn't remember her as vividly as she remembered me from school. What I knew was that I was at a good company, making good money doing, what I really wanted to do. I had a husband and a new baby, and

I was being offered a job with a company with no track record.

I went home and told my husband, sure we would share a laugh as the idea was preposterous.

"And?" he asked.

"And what?" I replied.

"Are you considering it?" He shocked me with this response. How could I just leave my job and begin traveling all over the U.S.? I had a child and a home and was starting to put down serious roots in the community.

He supported me, and so I began a new adventure. With each new change, I was soaring higher and higher in my life and career. I was introduced to contracting, small business, and healthcare. Everything I had done until that point in my profession created one more step forward. I leveraged my education, knowledge, and experience, which in turn opened up new opportunities for me.

After a little over three years, I was offered a leadership position with a large federal government contractor in healthcare. The division was responsible for various healthcare initiatives. After some time, the company was purchased by a larger company. This merger was lucrative for the employees and owners. I used the proceeds to move back to Hampton Roads, Virginia, near the area where I grew up. I had returned home, but I was a bigger and stronger person than when I left. I returned to my roots, not empty-handed; I was with a husband and two beautiful children and a third on the way.

Grow Where You Are Planted

I had flown a full circle in my life, except now I was ready to run my own company, ARDX. Each leap I made came with challenges, learning experiences, and growth. If I had not made those leaps, I would have been stuck in whatever position I decided to remain in. I was flying beyond the trees and soaring up the mountain, but I still had a bit more to go.

ARDX is a company that implements healthcare legislation and develops IT systems. The work we do is so essential and so fulfilling. Our company grew, and I knew I needed to up my game to meet the challenges of a company of 100 associates.

I had to step back a moment to see where we had grown, and what I needed to do to meet the next set of challenges so that we could build even more. I decided to return to school to get my Ph.D. in Business with a focus in Organizational Behavior.

With the help of my assistant, we found a school that met my requirements for being a robust, research-based program, surrounded by experienced executives. While it was like a needle in a haystack, she found it. However, there was one big challenge: it was at Oklahoma State University.

I had to travel once a month for the better part of a week. I started the program, and I had to read what felt like twenty journal articles a day. I was losing my mind. The professor told me that my job as a Ph.D. candidate was to find and close the gap in the literature. This meant I had to contribute something new in the area I was studying. It seemed like a monumental task.

After reading so many articles, I realized that there was a gap. I didn't see my story represented in the articles I was reading. I was looking for the story of my ascension from being this confused and frustrated child to soaring as a black butterfly defying all the odds.

Black Butterfly, sailed across the waters
tell your sons and daughters
what the struggle brings
Black Butterfly, set the skies on fire
rise up even higher
so the ageless winds of time can catch your
wings...

I talked to my dissertation committee chair about my thoughts. He gave me two theories that would change the course of my life: Dr. K. Anders Ericsson's "Expert Performance Theory" and "Deliberate Practice." Dr. Robert Baron and Rebecca A. Henry built on Ericsson's theory and asserted that vicarious learning and experiential learning could substitute for deliberate hands-on practice. We can learn by watching others and doing a task, rather than having to go through formal training. At that moment, I realized my research interest was not Organizational Development, rather, it was Entrepreneurship.

A lightbulb went off. I was a teacher. I could transfer what I had learned in my life to young girls. My idea was to go to forty-eight of the most impoverished communities in the U.S. and work with girls in middle school. What if I could teach these girls the skills of business and ignite their innovation and passion? They could become leaders and transform their communities from within. What if we could save these communities, one little girl at a time?

The Birth of Envision Lead Grow (ELG)

I developed a process to engage the girls that not only helped them in their quest to begin to think and act like businesswomen, but that was also observable and that I could track and gather data to analyze.

Leaning on the research of Baron and Henry, I developed a curriculum based on the eight components of deliberate practice. These components are:

1) highly demanding and require focused attention
2) designed around strengthening areas of weakness
3) repetitive
4) supported with continuous feedback

5) goal-oriented
6) infused with self-observation during activity
7) evaluated with self-reflection after completion
8) providing exertion over a long period (10,000 hours over ten years.)

We wanted to compress that time to help the girls reach expert performance. The research indicated that entrepreneurship uniquely involves activities identified in the deliberate practice model. In addition, the survival mode of living in the communities from which our young girls were drawn built in them the tenacity, resourcefulness, and self-control that could lead to improved deliberate practice performance.

In 2017, we began our tour and engaged 414 girls in these seven cities:

- ❖ Memphis, TN
- ❖ Greensboro, NC
- ❖ Atlanta, GA
- ❖ Baltimore, MD
- ❖ Philadelphia, PA
- ❖ Richmond, VA
- ❖ Norfolk, VA

We chartered a luxury bus with the ELG logo displayed on the side, and we took the program to the girls in the places they lived. We were immersed in their culture, as they became immersed in the entrepreneurial mindset. We saw and experienced many wonderful things on our journey.

I was unprepared for the emotions I would experience, but it became obvious on our first stop in Memphis. We were beginning a movement and I found myself standing in Lorraine Motel, the site where Dr. Martin Luther King Jr. was assassinated. I was in awe of his presence and his message of hope for the future. Now, I was beginning a similar journey.

Our next stop was Greensboro. North Carolina had become a familiar place to me, as my daughter was attending University of North Carolina in Chapel Hill. Greensboro is farther to the west, and as we passed by my daughter's school, I was struck by how lucky we were to have a partner like the University of North Carolina supporting our cause. The caliber of education and professionalism are second to none. When we arrived at UNC-Greensboro, they rolled out the red carpet for us, which was a very humbling experience.

To make our Atlanta stop a reality, we partnered with grassroots community leaders who connected us with the Butler Community Development Corporation. This organization has a rich history: it was known as the Black City Hall and was the center of the civil rights movement in Atlanta as well as the nation. It exists in one of the most impoverished parts of Atlanta, and so the girls that we attracted were ones in most need of hope and direction in their lives.

In Philadelphia, we were hosted by Temple University and met at the prestigious Fox School of Business, one of my choices for my doctoral degree. There was not the central contact for recruiting that we had in the other cities, and so we had to make connections with different organizations across the city. We were relieved that on the first day, girls showed up, and we were happy that our efforts had not been in vain.

In Baltimore we were hosted by Spark Baltimore, which is a cooperative space for entrepreneurs. When we stepped inside, the space exuded energy and innovation. They provided breakfast and lunch for the girls and provided entrepreneurs as speakers and judges. The entire experience was wonderful for the girls who attended and provided fertile soul in which they could bloom.

We were almost home when we arrived in Richmond, Virginia. We had logged thousands of miles by bus, and we were exhausted. I was having doubts about what I was doing and questioned my audacity to think I could pull it off and whether I could continue. Even the team who had travelled with me were getting irritated living with one another in Airbnbs for weeks.

1 Corinthians 10:13 says, "No temptation has overtaken you except what is common to mankind. And God is faithful; he will not let you be tempted beyond what you can bear. But when you are tempted, he will also provide a way out so that you can endure it."

Our way out came in the form of some of the best counselors (who were volunteers we had not met in person until we arrived) who brought renewed energy into our group. It was also time to take a break, and we celebrated our successes in downtown Richmond.

In *The Wizard of Oz*, Dorothy is told to close her eyes, click her heels three times, and say, "There is no place like home. There is no place like home." Returning to Norfolk on the last stop of our tour was my ruby slippers moment. We had the biggest week ahead of us with the largest number of girls, but as we rolled into town, we were revitalized. People in Norfolk had been following our progress through social media and were excited by our triumphant return.

Nancy Grnden, the executive director at the Strome Entreprenuerial Center at Old Dominion University, was one of our first and strongest supporters. She gave us total access to the resources at Old Dominion. The press was present, as were our families and biggest supporters for our big kickoff. There truly is no better place than home.

Everyone who participated that first year grew as individuals—the counselors, the mentors, the volunteers, the girls, and their families. One of the things we realized was that meeting the girls during a day camp was not the best plan. Many of the girls went home and then didn't return the next day for various reasons, primarily transportation. The ones who did had a different attitude after returning home. They were more cynical and had returned to a hopeless stance that no matter what they did, nothing would change. We knew we needed to make the first week in the program an overnight camp.

ELG evolved into a four-tier program that is free to the girls participating. It begins with a summer immersion program, which is a week-long sleep-away camp where the girls are given the foundations of becoming an entrepreneur. Many of the girls start the session as strangers and leave as great friends. Throughout the summer program, the girls take part in exercises to help them think bigger, to apply those ideas entrepreneurially, to use their STEAM (science, technology, engineering, art, and mathematics) skills in everyday life, and to make better decisions. At the end of the summer immersion camp, it is our hope that these young women leave with a solid business idea, a Passion Pitch they can use to sell their ideas to others, and confidence to take their company— and community—to the next level. They are given the opportunity at the end of the camp to pitch their ideas to a panel of judges. The winning venture receives $500 in seed money for her business.

Our new Girl Bosses return home, where they are paired with a local female mentor who works with them throughout their high school years to continue growing their business plans. The girls receive monthly guidance from our team via assignments.

In addition to the connection to their mentors through lessons, the girls connect through virtual meetings. We provide them with lessons and guidance on these calls, and the girls have a chance to interact and learn from one another.

It can be lonely to be in business for yourself, so Envision Lead Grow designed a way to ensure these young entrepreneurs never feel isolated. It is our belief that it is essential to have a network of support not only through an ELG branch city mentor but also other ELG peers and mentors from all branches.

The girls who remain in the program are invited to our Entrepreneur Institute, which is an all-expense-paid weekend in Washington, D.C. They work with Fortune 500 female executives and successful female entrepreneurs there.

The program is still young, and the data is being collected. After only one year in the program, our middle school-aged girls are running and growing profitable businesses. Once girls enter our program, they remain until they graduate high school, and then this cycle continues through college.

For many of our Girl Bosses, this is the first time they leave home, and 99% of the time, it is the first time they are exposed to a college campus. Many of the girls never even considered attending college; however, after only a week gaining some independence and having the seeds of success planted, they look forward to a bright future with a college degree on the horizon.

The Eight Seeds

I finally understood the beauty of the black butterfly. It can start so dark. When you look back over your life and see all the good and bad, understand its meaning and purpose, you can then soar as high as you can imagine, and even beyond.

We all have the power to solve problems, and we can take all those life lessons and begin to fuel innovation. I had been journaling for years as a business leader when I went back over my experiences and started noticing the patterns that led to my success. I took those themes and the components of deliberate practice and developed the curriculum titled the Eight Seeds of Success. This became the basis of the training the girls receive in the ELG program.

In just one week of working with these Girl Bosses, we could see the difference. We were providing them with what I hungered for as a child: a direction, an opportunity, and a tribe to support me. It was amazing the impact this had on these girls' mindset.

We were excited about the possibilities that having a mentor over the school year would unlock for these girls. To say that it has been a success would be a weak understatement. At the time of the writing of this book, we are in our third year. We have expanded the program into thirty states now. Our goal by 2020 is to be in forty-eight states and have one thousand girls in the program. We are well on our way.

I began this introduction as a little girl sitting alone in a living room, listening to records, imagining a world that I didn't know really existed.

One in which I belonged, was loved, and could grow a career and family. There were many challenges to that dream. My vision for ELG was to produce as perfect an incubator for entrepreneurs as I could. I want to minimize the obstacles and turn up the volume on the things that helped me.

At the end of *The Wizard of Oz*, Dorothy wakes up. She is not the same innocent girl she was before the storm. She looked at her world with new eyes and looked at her family and friends. Each of them was a character in her adventure. They represented heart, intellect, and courage.

I am bringing those lessons I have learned from my own journey to these girls. I'm providing them direction, education, and mentors. All of these were components of my own success.

Many of these girls are in their own dark cocoon. I don't want barriers such as having limited access to learning, money, or mentors keep them in that darkness any longer. I want them to emerge early, go to college, and discover the leader--the black butterfly--that already exists within them.

We can do this by helping increase high school graduation success rates. We can decrease the number of teenage pregnancies. We teach them the benefits of delayed gratification.

Overview of the 8 Seeds of Success

The rest this book is dedicated to the 8 Seeds of Success that are the curriculum and basis of what is taught in ELG. These Seeds not only apply to business or careers, but also to how we live our lives. These Seeds are intended to shift minds toward success in all aspects of our lives so that we can live a balanced life. So that we can soar to ever-higher heights.

Seed #1: What Makes Your Heart Sing. Consider what brings you joy or peace. When I was a child, in addition to listening to music, I loved to dance. I was happiest when I danced—any kind of dancing would do. As I got older, I found happiness in so many other things, like traveling and writing. I found that there were some aspects that I really liked in my work life: planning, training, and mentoring. I also really like solving problems and finding new ways for clients to succeed. I took these things that made me happy and found a way to use them in my daily life. It is what brings me joy.

Seed #2: Put Pen to Paper. I love the feeling of setting a goal and writing it down. For me, that act of putting pen to paper crystallizes my dream into a goal and makes it all the more real. I keep a journal with me at all times. People wonder what I'm writing about. The truth is, sometimes they are random thoughts, and other times they are detailed plans.

Seed #3: Speak It and Bring it to Life. Speak as if it is. I recently met a new entrepreneur, and she introduced herself as an itty, bitty business owner working out of her basement with no customers. I quickly told her that this would be her elevator speech: "I'm the owner of a successful venture, working out of my office, catering to my customer base." Don't reinforce negativity by speaking down on yourself; speak your successes into existence.

Seed #4: Inhale and Exhale. Determine who breathes life into it and who drains the energy out of it. It's commonly said that you are the average of the five people you spend the most time with. If the people in your inner circle don't believe in your dreams, soon enough, you won't either. If they just agree with everything you say without working for growth, soon your own growth will cease as well. It's all about finding the balance of people who are invested in you enough to give you valuable feedback that will help you excel.

Seed #5: Delve into the Details. The devil is in the details. You have to be willing to dig in and get dirty to make sure your dream will grow. You need the facts and figures so you can chart a successful path.

Seed #6: Plan your Success. It is so easy to jump in and get to work, but the magic is in the plan. Zig Ziglar said, "Success occurs when opportunity meets preparation." Plan your dream so that when the window of opportunity presents itself to you, you are ready to turn that window into a door.

Seed #7: Reevaluate your Plan. It is never too late to modify your vision. Every day is a chance to learn and to adjust. I'm always analyzing new data that can cause detours and pivots in my plans. Do not continue on a path of destruction just because it is the path you started on. Reevaluate and make sure you are going to where you want to go.

Seed #8: Stop and Smell the Roses from the Seeds You Planted. Ahhhhh...the joy of success! You deserve to take some time to enjoy what you have created. It is your baby. Marvel at how it has grown!

Chapter Two

What Makes Your Heart Sing?

I RECALL SITTING on a panel at a Virginia Governor's Small Business conference. I learned that my company was considered a "two-percenter." What this meant was that less than 2% of businesses listed in the North American Industry Classification System (NAICS) Codes employ more than fifty people. My company employed over one hundred. That means 98% of the companies in the US are small businesses with fewer than forty-nine employees. The vast majority of those small businesses were solopreneurs, meaning companies made up of a single entrepreneur. This statistic surprised me.

There was a man on the panel who said that his passion was making money. He believed that money solved problems. His words got me thinking. I know money is important to a business, but is it the most important thing? I start from a place of passion and it has always served me well. Which comes first: passion or money? Do we need money to drive a company and through our success we become passionate? Or does passion drive the company to be successful and therefore generate revenue? I subscribe to the latter.

Our experiences inform our perspective. As an entrepreneur, I've experienced many dark days. There were days when associates came in with their own life problems. Because I was leading the organization, I felt responsible for solving them. This took me off-target for what I wanted to accomplish that day, week, month, or even year. I was still liable for overhead, payroll, and all the other aspects of running a business.

It was during those challenging times when the pressure was on, and I felt the weight of the world on my shoulders, that I relied on my passion to carry me. If I didn't have passion for the work, and passion for the people who worked for me, I would've given up many times. It would have been the natural thing to do. My passion kept me fired up and gave me the energy to keep going.

Money alone cannot get you through tough times. When passion burns within us, it drives our creativity and our ability to problem solve. Money alone doesn't erase the emotional responsibility of leading and guiding an organization. Having passion for what I do, and the purpose of my company fuels my creative juices to problem solve and allows me to see the high roads even when everyone around me sees the low ones.

Those days, I had to remember what made my heart sing. What makes life feel lighter for me? What makes me stay positive and see the silver lining during times of turmoil? That's the driving force that keeps me going every day.

I am proud to say that over the years ARDX has been awarded over a hundred million dollars in federal government contracts, but that isn't what makes my heart sing. We are in the center of healthcare in the United States. The work we do affects whether seniors have a benefit called "Medicare Part C." We influence the government to offer drug benefits to seniors and people with disabilities. We were on the front line of President Obama's Affordable Care Act. Because of what we do, today, a mother of five with cancer can continue to receive healthcare benefits even though she has a pre-existing medical condition.

That's what makes my heart sing: because I know what I do *matters*. It took me half of my life to figure that out. As I mentioned in Chapter 1, I spent years in a restrictive cocoon, and even when I began to emerge, it took me years to find the path that made my heart sing and my spirit soar. I was proud of what I had accomplished with my company. Because of my passion, I was employing others, which enabled my associates to have a career in which they could have upward mobility and create a legacy for their families.

To me, the concept of community has been a core value in everything I do; it's embedded in my DNA. When I first started ARDX, I wanted to include the community in our practices. We developed a corporate responsibility program, and it was through this program that we decided to create "healthcare academies." These are free community health education programs. In them, we discussed health and nutrition to reduce obesity in children. We gave them information on healthy eating habits and exercise. We also wanted to provide education and awareness for women, so we developed "Women's Wellness Celebrations." We held events in which anywhere from two hundred to four hundred women attended and learned the importance of taking care of their physical health and wellness. In 2019, we served over 1500 women and 3000 children at no cost to their families or community.

In 2018, we launched The ARDX Foundation, which focuses on shining a light on mental wellness.

Our mission is to remove the stigma of mental challenges and normalize the conversation. I have been very blessed to be working on healthcare legislation while being able to connect with the community and provide education. I brought my joy to my company. I have been fortunate to be on the legislative side of medical insurance and that allowed me to dive deeper and help people in need in a more direct way.

It's a process of self-discovery, and there were many times I could have settled in my life. I could have stayed in a job because it was safe, even though I wasn't passionate about it. I would have missed the opportunity to make a difference in the world and to have such a significant impact on the lives of so many. By discovering what I was passionate about, my heart became full. The success of my business and career are the results of living in my passion zone.

First Day at Envision Lead Grow (ELG)

In the introduction of our ELG program, I mention my first mentor and how she sat me down in her office and talked to me about the way I dressed. I carried her feedback throughout my career, so I wanted to instill the importance of dressing for success with the girls from day one.

The girls participating in ELG were instructed to dress to impress. We didn't set any stringent requirements. I knew many of these girls didn't have the money to go and buy expensive clothes, but I wanted them to dress as neatly as they could to represent themselves well. I wanted them to take the program seriously, and at the same time, I wanted them to develop a sense of pride in themselves.

I remember this little girl in her impeccably neat dress on the first day of ELG in Memphis. Her hair was meticulously parted in the middle, and she had two big afro-puffs on top.

"How did you find us?" she asked. "Nothing good ever comes to Memphis."

My heart melted on the spot. It was an immediate validation that I was exactly where I needed to be. My mission was that by the end of the week, these girls would know that not only did something good come to Memphis, but someone great lives in Memphis.

That week we learned through the girls' stories that the issue affecting them most was the gangs in their communities. Each of their lives was surrounded by violence. One of the girls shared that her mother told her that if she was ever going to make something of herself, she needed to move far away from Memphis. We discussed this. If everyone successful left the area, who was going to lead the next generation?

At the end of the week, the girls were able to pitch their ideas for a company they'd like to create to a panel of mentors and people in their community. Their average age was about ten years old. Each of them stood on stage in front of business leaders and pitched their ideas. Just having the courage to speak to adults in that way, in a three-minute speech, already made them successful.

Something extraordinary happened in those five days we spent together at ELG Camp. Each of the girls who stood on that stage incorporated into their pitch something they were going to do to help THEIR CITY. We ignited passion and innovation in those girls.

I left this event in tears. My heart was full. Each one of those little girls was me. Many of the moms present were also single moms, each struggling, trying to raise their children the best way they could. I saw so much hope in their faces when they hugged me that I knew we had brought them something priceless.

This tour of eight cities was the beginning of my Ph.D. dissertation, and I was focused on getting it done. I had not dreamed that ELG could have such a significant impact on these girls and their communities. I was onto something big that I needed to grow beyond my paper.

It makes my heart sing every time I hear a little girl change their "I can't" into an "I can" and "I will." My heart sings every time I get an email from a parent who says their child was transformed because of ELG. Their children have new goals and a new outlook on life.

I honestly believe you can't be what you can't see.

Many of these girls are being raised by an aunt or a grandmother. I can share with these girls my experience. I know what the feelings of isolation and dissociation from my parents felt like. I couldn't imagine back then that the cocooned life I endured as a child could be the tool to connect me to other girls' lives. That pain allowed me to step into their space with understanding and show them the way out.

My mission is to be a positive, shiny object for those girls. When you are living in poverty, you pay attention to the shiny things other people have: their expensive cars, their clothes, their shoes. Often, kids will follow those people and end up doing something harmful. I want to be the positive shiny thing for these girls and show them a path that leads to more significant outcomes.

Case Study: Azaria

When we grow older, we still have an inner child, a playful spirit full of hope, wonder, and creativity locked inside us. I have met many women who wait their entire lives to begin to let their inner child loose. Many people believe you must follow a specific path to become responsible. That following the dreams of our youth is somehow irresponsible. The truth is, we don't have to wait. We can start transforming our ideas into reality at any age. Azaria, one of the Girls Bosses in the ELG program, is an excellent example of this.

Azaria was raised by her mom, a young single mother, and always had a STEM (Science, Technology, Engineering, and Math) passion. She wanted to know how things worked in the world, and Azaria was fortunate enough to go to a school where there was an active STEM program. During her 5th grade year, she was accepted into a special middle school elsewhere. She realized that not only was she leaving the school she had been attending for six years, as well as all of her teachers and friends, but she'd also leave the STEM program she loved so much.

From a non-Title One school, Azaria was moving to a Title One school—a school where at least fifty percent of the children are on the free lunch program—with a challenging curriculum. This new program allowed her to earn high school credits. It was a great opportunity. But Azaria missed being around peers who looked like her and shared her loved for STEM. She became discouraged when someone at school said, "Black girls don't like science." It hurt her because she loved science. Those words challenged her passion and her sense of self.

Azaria was shy and didn't engage much with her peers in her new environment. Her mother gave her a brochure about our ELG summer camp, and at first, Azaria was hesitant. She didn't feel she would fit in, but she went anyway.

Within the first day at ELG, Azaria was hooked! She felt encouraged and found a tribe of girls just like her. My story resonated with her because she also came from a single-mom family.

Azaria overcame her shyness quickly because she was involved in activities in which she had to speak to others. Her confidence grew as the week progressed. She remembers the exact turning point for her. "We had to do pitches on the final day. I was nervous, but I remember the program manager telling us that we were going to do great. That we could do it. That stuck with me."

Azaria was only twelve when she attended her first ELG camp. Over the past three years, she has participated in three ELG camps and two institutes in DC. Her passion was ignited! Because she wanted to share her love for STEM with other girls, she created a non-profit company called Zinc Girlz (zincgirlz.org). Its mission:

ZincGirlz allows inner-city girls to explore STEM through various enrichment activities and experiments. In addition to learning about STEM, girls are also encouraged to love themselves, obtain higher education, and engage in community service projects.

Since she started the non-profit three years ago, Azaria has worked with over one hundred girls. She's overcome her shyness and now does public speaking engagements on STEM for girls. She feels that ELG was the jumping-off point in her life. Azaria was chosen as a participant in the Disney Dreamers Academy with Steve Harvey and Essence Magazine for her phenomenal work.

But Azaria wasn't the only one inspired by the program.

Azaria's mother has been involved in the non-profit as well and is one of her biggest supporters. According to Azaria, her mother was so inspired by my story that she has gone back to school to get her master's degree in Social Work.

Azaria hopes to build a legacy that helps girls become involved in STEM. She wants to create something lasting, with an impact that extends beyond her time.

Showing Up In My Life

When I began ARDX, it grew quickly. I made some big mistakes along the way, but I learned from them. While it was not my first entrepreneurial endeavor, it was my first time building a company with a number of associates who relied on me and the company's success. As it developed, I felt isolated and lonely at the top. I wanted to surround myself with family and friends who could help me. I needed people I trusted to help me in the growth phase.

My husband was running a successful fitness company at the time, and I asked him to put his work there on hold and help me with mine. I needed him in the back office supporting and helping me with some of the day-to-day operations. I see now how unfair that was to him.

He wasn't used to working in an office. He was active and was used to spending his days doing physical activity. He was making the sacrifice for me, but he became a caged bird. He had to sit at a desk all day crunching numbers, and he was miserable. That created a lot of pressure on our relationship. At the time, I couldn't see the toll it was taking on him and our marriage. I was in so deep with my company that the demands and pressure on both of us were unrelenting.

I've always believed in the sanctity and wholeness of my family. As I felt that promise begin to slip, I had to take a step back and evaluate what I needed to do to serve both my business *and* my family.

I realized I had targeted people I trusted to help me. I had chosen them regardless of whether the task I was asking them to perform was in their skillset or even something they wanted to do. They came to help out of their love for me. But it takes more than just love to grow a company. I had to learn the lesson of skill versus will. My family and friends were willing to help me, but that did not mean they had the skills I needed. Over time I was able to hire key people with the skills I needed, and I was fortunate that they also had the passion, and will I needed to push forward.

This was not the only challenge I had in my life as my company created more demand. My life began to slip out of balance. It's taken me years to set things right.

As a wife and a mother, I had to learn to pick my battles more carefully. I needed to focus on the most important things and people in my life. I had to reimagine my work/life balance. I discovered that I can't be everything to everybody. And I can't be everywhere at the same time. I couldn't be at every soccer game my kids had. I couldn't make all the school plays or teacher's conferences I was expected to be at. I was having a flashback to my childhood: I was turning into a provider and losing my role as a nurturer.

When I began to hire associates, I made a commitment to them. I made a promise to them that I had to keep, which also meant I needed to make sacrifices in my personal life.

Because I was raised by a single mom who couldn't be there for most of my youth activities, I had promised myself that I would be there for my children. At times, I even became resentful of my husband because he was able to be there for my children more often than I was. He had more freedom and more availability than I did.

There is a line when you are a business owner. It is the line between you and the business. When you are a solo-prenuer or when your company is small, the line does not really exist. You are the company. If you are not working, the company is not working. As a company begins to grow, you can begin to develop that line and allow others to help you run the company so that you have more control of your time and schedule. I had to figure that out and partner with my husband and those I worked with so that I could shift some time back to my family.

I knew I wanted and needed to be a better wife and a better mother. These passions are just as important, or more, than my love for my career. To accomplish this, I had to think differently.

When ARDX was ready to expand from one building to two, I decided to build a suite for myself and my family. In the center of the suite is my office. On each side of the office are French doors. On one side is a conference room where I have business meetings, and on the other side is a living room with sofas and a TV. They have access to a microwave and a fridge. This is the area where my family and I can interact.

Oprah had a show for a while called *Behind the Scenes*. I just loved the furniture and the setup she had: dainty furniture, bright colors, a comfortable, welcoming space. I think I may have done my job too well because I had more than person ask me why I went home when I had created a second home in my office.

The kids can do homework there, relax, and have snacks. When they are sick, they can lie on the sofa, and we have covers for them to snuggle under. It allows me to be nurturing and nurse them back to health. I moved them to a new school, so they are only two minutes away from the office. Because I was across the street from the school, I was able to volunteer more. I wanted to be there watching my children while they were in the water. I found a way for me to be a mom. It's a vital role for me, and my heart could sing because now I could be present.

Take Action

Our desire to explore, create, sacrifice, and overcome our obstacles is fueled by passion. Any endeavor worth pursuing requires passion as its first building block. We must enter every new venture knowing that it must appeal to one of our primary passions.

The discovery of our passion involves identifying the things that make us happiest. When I was a child, I loved dancing and was happiest when I danced—any kind of dancing would do. As I got older, I discovered happiness in so many other things, like traveling and writing. When my career began, I took a deep pleasure in aspects of my work life such as planning, training, and mentoring. Through introspection, I was able to look beyond the surface of what made me happy, discovering what I could do to build my legacy. To pursue our purpose, we must recognize and understand what drives us as individuals.

My mother taught me how to plan for the future. She would sit me down at the dining room table with a chart she had made and ask me, "What do you want to accomplish by the time you are fourteen? Fifteen?" And so on. For each of these ages, she had columns for wealth, family, education, and more. I used this chart to set my goals all the way through my twenties. Back then, I already knew I wanted a doctorate even though I wasn't sure what it was. One of the goals I set for myself every year was that I wanted to make money, my age plus $5,000 (at fourteen that would have been $19,000).

Having something visual and tangible was powerful. At ELG camp, one of the activities I have the girls do is a Passion Board. They are given magazines, scissors, and glue to create a board that represents not only their passion but also a vision of their future.

Activities:

1. Identify the activities and dreams that bring you happiness and satisfaction.

2. Be willing to look beyond pursuits that bring you short moments of gratification. Pour your effort into finding the gifts that breathe life into your purpose and add to your legacy.

3. Build your passion board (instructions below).

Passion Boards can help you uncover clues you can use to learn about your interests. They help you start to understand what you might want to do as a professional. It isn't only for girls to dream about the future; it's also a lens into our past to remember what our dreams were. A Passion Board can also help you figure out a business idea and build a plan to make it happen. Our passion is made up of the things that make our hearts sing! Once you figure out your passions, you can build a plan that lets you spend as much time with them as possible.

a.   Draw four squares like the one in Figure 1 below. Clear your mind and think big thoughts. In your dreams, what do you want for your future?

b.   In the top left corner of your passion board, write down the things you see for your brightest, most successful future. For instance, you could write, "In my brightest future, I want to own a chain of custom stuffed animal shops, where everyone can build the stuffed animal they've always dreamed of."

c. In the top right section, write about where you are now. For example, "I own six stuffed animals, but I don't know how they were made. I live near a store that sells custom teddy bears. I've only seen a sewing machine once, and I don't know how to turn it on."

d. In the bottom left box, write about the tools you'll need to get to the big dream you wrote about in the top left box. "I'll need a sewing machine, lots of different materials like fur & feathers, and buttons, lots of buttons."

e.   In the bottom right box, think about the people you will help, the lives that will change because of your custom stuffed animals. Maybe you'll donate some to the local children's hospital or create an "adopt a stuffed duck" charity to help less fortunate kids.

Here is the fun part. For each section, find pictures on the web or in magazines that remind you of the things you wrote and add them to each section on the board. Once you've finished, put your Passion Board where you can view it daily. It can be at your desk or next to your bathroom mirror. It can be wherever you can see it and pause to think about your passion and how you can fill your day with it.

Developing
A Passion Board

What I envision for the future

Where I Am Right Now

Tools I Need to Get Where I want to Go

Who Will I Help Once I Get There

Developing
A Passion Board

Chapter Three

Put Pen to Paper

I'M THE TYPE of person who is always moving forward. As soon as I'm finished with one project, my brain is on to the next. At any given time, I have competing thoughts in my brain, and I've found that instead of stressing out about forgetting something, I write it down. By writing information down, I'm able to purge it from my mind and open my brain to new ideas. It is similar to uploading information to the cloud for storage. It provides more memory on the computer. Writing things down unclutters our minds, which allows us to be more creative and focused, while at the same time giving us the peace of mind that the information will not be lost and forgotten.

Also, there is something very cathartic about writing things down. Nothing is more satisfying than that sound of a sharpened No.2 pencil on paper. Writing things down brings more permanence to an idea. It brings it from just an idea floating around our brains to the real world in which we can then share that idea with others.

Our Experiences Create Our Reality

In my early years, I enjoyed watching soap operas in the afternoons. The images I saw influenced my vision of the world. They helped me develop my goals for the future; they fed my vision. I remember watching the story of Angie and Jessie on *General Hospital.* This was what I thought I wanted my marriage and life to be like. Even the show *The Jeffersons* had an influence. I wanted that penthouse and to live a sophisticated life. One of my favorite shows, and perhaps the one that had the most significant influence over the structure and culture of ARDX, was *Designing Women.* I loved the idea of a house environment for a business and appreciated the strong female characters and their entrepreneurial spirit. I loved the decor, the interactions between them, and the camaraderie that existed. It gave me a feeling of warmth and a sense of unity. These became goals that followed me years later into my business and personal life.

I was able to take that vision of my youth and transform it into reality. My first office for ARDX was a two-story condo with an open floor plan (very much like the set of *Designing Women*). Starting out, we even had four women working, just like the show. I had a vision, but I had not really worked it all out or written down what I really wanted. The women who were working with me had some major challenges in their lives: they were dealing with divorce, death of a loved one, and some other heavy issues. All these major life stressors existing at the same time became a recipe for disaster. What I really wanted in the office was unity: all of us working together with a common vision, supporting each other with our strengths. I had to alter my vision and decide what I really wanted, and how to achieve it. I needed to write it down and create a plan.

Having a clear vision is important, but it will remain just a vision if we don't commit it to paper. We can not only write about our life and business goals, but we can also figure out the steps we need to take along the way. Our triumphs. Our joys. Our sorrows. Our missteps.

The great thing about a pencil that makes it different from a pen is that it has two ends; it has an eraser. Our goal planning does not need to be chiseled in stone. Our goals often shift and change, and like my first office experiment, a vision might not work out quite the way we thought it would. We can just turn the pencil over, erase the past, and begin writing our new plan.

Vision Statements

When we write things down, we not only make a permanent record of our thoughts and ideas, but we create a way to be accountable. By writing our ideas down we are able to share those ideas with others, and then we are accountable to make those words a reality.

When we commit to our goals on paper, we call these vision statements. These are the items we hope to achieve and the standards by which we live. Writing out our vision statement helps us stay on track, and it can be a tool for others to rally around. It becomes the gold standard. Decisions and future goals grow from that vision statement. When we share it with others, they can then hold us accountable, because we have made it a permanent promise.

Vision statements can change over time as we grow and mature, and as our values and interests change. You need to take out that eraser and be prepared to rewrite your life script, and then be prepared to share it with others. Remember the act of sharing what you have written adds an important layer of accountability.

I've had several different vision statements in my life. The current vision statement in my life is: "I live a life of service and excellence that leaves a legacy for my children and for generations to come."

Other very successful leaders have created personal vision statements which they have shared with the world.

"I want to be a teacher. I want to be known for inspiring my students to be more than they thought they could be." Oprah Winfrey

"To serve as a leader, live a balanced life, and apply ethical principles to make a significant difference." Denise Morrison, CEO of the Campbell Soup Company

"To have fun in [my] journey through life and learn from [my] mistakes." Sir Richard Branson, Founder of the Virgin Group

"I define personal success as being consistent to my own personal mission statement: to love God and love

others." Joel Manby, CEO of Herschend Family Entertainment

"To use my gifts of intelligence, charisma, and serial optimism to cultivate the self-worth and net-worth of women around the world." Amanda Steinberg, Founder of Dailyworth.com

Vision Statements for Organizations

Vision statements can be for companies, but first we should write them for ourselves. When we know what we personally aspire to, then we can create something larger. It's from this core vision that we can begin building something more substantial, such as a company or other types of organizations.

Once we have created our personal vision statement, we can take the core components and begin to build the foundation of our business. Companies create vision statements to drive the company forward. Creating our statement first helps us become clear on our "why". In the case of ARDX, I was clear that I needed to be in a position of "service." Here is the vision statement for ARDX:

Mission
ARDX's mission is to improve the quality, efficiency, and effectiveness of healthcare for our nation's most vulnerable populations.

Vision
ARDX will be the most trusted advisor in navigating the nation's evolving healthcare challenges by consistently providing innovative and efficient solutions and unique overall client experience in the areas of Population Health, Payment Reform, and Patient-Centered Care & Outcomes.

Values
Integrity, Integration, Innovation, Inspiration, and Individuality.

We decided recently to rework and rethink the ARDX vision statement. We took out our pencils, opened our minds, and created:

We strive to be our customers' first choice when delivering the nation's healthcare solutions.

Investing myself in ELG was easy because the purpose of ELG is congruent with the vision and mission of my own life. When we sat down and created the vision statement for ELG, I had a strong sense of the "why" of the organization. Here is the vision for ELG:

To transform communities of poverty into communities of prosperity through the power and promise of middle school girls.

SMART Goals

Once we have created our vision statement, we need a strategy for achieving that vision. It has to be more than pretty words on paper hanging on the wall. Creating a strategy for making your vision reality begins with setting goals. Again, goals are only ideas until they are written down. It is time to sharpen our pencils, get to work, and create goals that others can rally around, hold each other accountable to, and execute.

Imagine walking into an IKEA. It is this big warehouse of furniture and at every turn there is a room set up. These are meant to create a vision: something we can look at, walk around, and envision in our minds. You are given paper and a small sharp pencil to write down the items you want to purchase for your home. Eighteen hours later, you find your way out of the maze and are ready to make your purchases.

You have written your vision statement and intentions. They have to align with the vision of your home and its overall theme.

There is a long corridor. You begin to pick up items to take them to the checkout and make your purchase. On your way, you are surrounded by candy and other small decor that magically makes its way into your cart.

You make your purchase and take it home. It is here that the dream of a cute little nightstand can become a nightmare of screws and small pieces of wood. Hopefully, someone in the family likes to read instructions in Swedish, and the process of putting it together is not too difficult.

In companies, this is where some people get into trouble. They don't have a set of instructions (goals) for achieving their vision (cute little nightstand). They try to execute without planning and find instead that they have created a cat box, with six screws left over.

Creating clear goals helps you to make your vision into a reality. They must be clear and something that others can read and readily understand (even if they don't speak Swedish).

While he was not the inventor of SMART goals, Robert S. Rubin, a professor from Saint Louis University, wrote about them in an article for The

Society of Industrial and Organizational Psychology. Here is how he explained the acronym:

- ❖ Specific (simple, sensible, significant)
- ❖ Measurable (meaningful, motivating)
- ❖ Achievable (agreed, attainable)
- ❖ Relevant (reasonable, realistic, and resourced, results-based)
- ❖ Time-bound (time-based, time/cost limited, timely, time-sensitive)

Using this acronym will help you develop clear, concise, and understandable goals. I used SMART when developing the structure of ELG. After the dissertation phase was over, we needed to develop goals so ELG could become a viable organization. Let me tell you how we chose those goals and how they fit into our overall ELG plan:

Specific. The goals you write should be clear and concise. They should be easy to understand and in their purest form, without complicated words or phrases. Use the five "W" questions to make your goals specific.

- ❖ Who is involved?
- ❖ Why is the goal important?
- ❖ What is it you want to accomplish?
- ❖ Where is the goal located?

❖ Which resources will be needed to accomplish your goal?

In ELG, we were extremely specific about what we wanted to accomplish: We will reach 1,000 girl-bosses in 48 states by 2020.

It doesn't have to be any more complicated than that. We knew we needed funding and volunteers. Since I was providing the bulk of the funding, I began to assemble a larger team to help me reach that goal.

Measurable. If you can't see it, hear it, feel it, taste it, smell it, or touch it, how will it help you accomplish your goal? It has to be observable and measurable. Ask yourself:

❖ How does something need to happen?
❖ How many of something will you need?
❖ How will you know when you've accomplished your goal?
❖ Does your goal interact with one or more of your five senses?

Making a goal measurable helps you stay on track and stay motivated. Can you imagine following a race with your eyes closed and your ears plugged? How would you know when the race started or ended? Much of the excitement of a race is witnessing what happens on the track as it occurs.

Goals are the same way. When you can observe them, you become more excited as you see yourself getting close to the finish line. It helps push you forward.

In our specific ELG goal statement, we describe the number of girls, the number of states, and the time frame in which we wanted to accomplish that goal.

Achievable. We all have grand ideas of where we want to be, who we want to be with, and what we'd like to create. Aim high but be realistic. If you are starting a business and you set a goal of making over a million dollars in the first year, this may be an impossible goal to achieve. That's not to say that you can't work to the million-dollar mark, but you may want to set smaller stepping-stone goals to get there. With each achievement, you can turn up the heat and set a greater and more audacious goal for yourself.

To determine whether your goal is achievable or not, ask yourself:

- ❖ How will you accomplish your goal?
- ❖ What constraints make the goal more challenging to achieve?

We knew from our first tour with ELG that the program was viable. With time we've become more confident that we'll definitely reach our goal. In 2018 we had 250 girls go through the program in nine states. In 2019 we had 600 girls in 30 states. We are sure we are going to be in 48 states by 2020 while hitting our 1000-girl goal.

Relevant. The goals you set should be things you are passionate about and that matter to you. They should be relevant to your life. Each goal should be in harmony with the next one. Take control of your goals, even though you have others around you providing support. At the end of the day, they are still *your* goals, and *you* are responsible for taking them across the finish line.

Ask yourself the questions below to determine if your goal is relevant:

- Is your goal worthy of your time, attention, and sweat equity?
- Is the timing right to start working on your goal?
- Is your goal in alignment with your other goals and other people's goals around you?
- Is this your dream, your passion, and are you the right person to achieve this goal?

This was perhaps the most natural step for me in determining my ELG SMART goals. Not only was I passionate about what we were achieving, but I had surrounded myself with a team and board that was equally as passionate about my ELG vision.

Time-Bound. Many studies say putting a time limit on your goals makes them more likely to get accomplished. It creates a level of accountability that can help fight procrastination. Having a time limit enables you to put short-term goals ahead of long-term ones.

Add an expiration date to your goals to make them time sensitive:
- ❖ By when do you want to accomplish your goal?
- ❖ How long should it take you to reach it?
- ❖ What part of the goal should you be accomplishing each day?

I want to reach 1,000 girls in 48 states by 2020. Once we achieve that goal, we will be setting even more substantial and more audacious goals for the future.

Staying on Track

By creating SMART goals, you can begin to see results. With each goal achieved, you should have a mini celebration. You can take a moment to recognize where you've come from, where you are now, and where you want to be in the future. It creates hope and makes our path forward more precise and the journey more comfortable.

There are different ways to monitor and control goals. The important thing is that you have a process. It should be one that assists you daily rather than something you look at once a month or even once a year. If you do not monitor what is going on, issues can draw you away from your goals and consume your attention.

When you monitor your goals, you can assess your progress. You should answer these questions:

❖ Is this goal going to happen this year?
❖ Or, is there some part of the goal that is attainable this year?

You can break your goal down into smaller, attainable steps. Accomplishing these smaller steps will give you a sense of success.

I can look at the end of the day, the week, and the year, and witness that I have moved a step closer to reaching my vision.

These steps work for company goals as well as personal ones. From the beginning, we've had an annual meeting at ARDX where we've created a company roadmap for the upcoming year. Our roadmap has three main goals. Underneath each of these goals are the eight or nine strategic steps we need to take to reach those goals.

We look at each major goal from three different perspectives: financial, customer, internal processes. We associate an action from each perspective for each goal.

Then, each of the senior leaders in the company takes on one of the goals. They champion it to make sure their goal is achieved. Those leaders are not only responsible for executing on the goal, but their compensation is also linked to their achieving the goal.

The three Ps—People, Processes, and Performance—are the drivers. This can be summed up as People + Processes = Performance. The three Ps help the leaders—and those they lead—meet their assigned goals. Those larger goals then cascade down to the next leader level. Those employees take a goal, and so forth, until everyone has a goal they are going to achieve for that year.

During our monthly meetings, each leader reports on their progress in achieving their assigned goal. It's so important to check in and share how things are progressing. This way, there's not only accountability, but they can also present their challenges to other leaders for ideas and support. We have report cards, from the top-level positions down to the line workers, to hold employees accountable for their success. These scorecards are a road map. Remember the grid I described above with the goals and the four perspectives? When we review our progress, we tag each perspective with a red, yellow, or green mark.

Green: Everything is progressing, and there are no apparent issues.

Yellow: There's a risk that needs to be mediated. (This is a warning before they become problems.)

Red: There are definite issues to work out.

The Contract

I met my husband the first day I was on campus at James Madison University (JMU). My mother and my boyfriend at the time came to help me move in. There was a gentleman from Omega Psi Phi fraternity whose community service project was to help freshman girls move into the dorm. I know what you are thinking. To this day, I question the validity of who that community service act was actually serving. That boy who helped us years later became my husband.

I remember my mother commenting in the elevator how nice the boy was, which was a little off-putting because I already had a boyfriend to whom I was committed. My boyfriend and I met up during weekends and for the holidays. But over time, the pressures of school and my desire to be closer to the people on campus who I considered my tribe finally dissolved my long-distance relationship.

About nine months later, I agreed to go on a date with my now-husband. I've always been a very forthright and practical woman. After two months of serious dating, I wanted to know what his intentions were because I was on a mission and had a roadmap. I couldn't be distracted. I needed someone who would support me in my goals and vision. I was clear on what I wanted to achieve in my life and the mile markers that I needed to make along the way. I was like the conductor of a train; I had to keep a tight schedule to make it to the train stops on time. I had to arrive on time and leave on time. I could not have any unnecessary distractions to take me off the rails.

So, I created a contract. Not some simple verbal promise or empty platitude. I wrote up a formal relationship contract and presented it to him to sign. I needed to know that he intended to marry me. My standards were high, and I didn't want any "players." I needed his life vision and my life vision to align.

He signed the contract. I had no idea whether he would honor it or not, as people's lives and journeys change, but at least it might give him a second to pause and think. There is something formal and permanent to a written contract that people take more seriously than a verbal commitment.

My husband is four years older than I am. When I gave him the contract, in my 18-year-old mind, I thought that a 22-year-old should already know what they wanted to do in life. That he should have it all figured out. But who really knows where they are in their life at that age? Unbeknownst to me, he did commit to marrying me but had no intention of doing it until he was at least 30. This was precisely how old he was when we finally walked down the aisle together.

My husband graduated before me and decided to enlist in the military while I continued my journey at JMU. First, he was stationed in South Carolina, North Carolina, Georgia, and eventually in California. During this period there were a number of breakups and makeups. When he was transferred to California, I told him that I didn't want to live that far away from home. We had a contract to be married, but the move delayed that contract for a year.

The delay could've been a year or two, but that's not what mattered to me. I knew with that contract, and our mutual commitment to it, I was at least on the path to be married to him. We had a plan.

Life doesn't just happen. We had a lot of work to do, and sacrifices to make, to achieve the goals we had set for ourselves. It's a highly active process. At times you must delay gratification because you have to focus on the big picture.

So, while it didn't happen in the exact time frame, I wanted it to happen, overall, we stuck to the contract. I knew I wanted a family, and I knew I wanted multiple children who were relatively close in age. After I moved in with my mother, for the rest of my childhood I grew up as an only child, and I didn't want to replicate the loneliness I experienced growing up with my own children. That's why I had specific dates I wanted to be married by and begin to have children. This was my "Jesse and Angie" marriage idea. This was my vision. I had developed a strategy for achieving it, and I prayed his vision would join with mine. Fortunately, the contract was finally met with an "I do."

Contracts at Home

From the beginning of our marriage, my husband and I have had a weekly family business meeting. We would meet after church, and we took it very seriously. We had an agenda, minutes, and we would talk about our goals.

At first, I wanted to buy a home for our family. I didn't care what kind of house it was; it could be a condo or townhome. I just knew the importance of home ownership. My husband wanted to wait and save for a single-family home. We were living in a lovely new apartment at the time, but we knew that if we really wanted a home, we were going to have to save as much money as possible.

Initially, we moved into the house where he'd grown up. His parents had moved to a new home and let us rent the house for cheap. We stayed there for a year and saved for our down payment. As soon as our first child was born, we moved into a home that we had built.

We had applied the concepts of SMART goals to achieve our dream of being in our own home within two years:

❖ **Specific:** We decided we wanted a home in an area where we could raise our kids. We also needed a home where we could raise more than one child. We knew what we wanted in the house.

❖ **Measurable**: We knew how much money we needed to raise to have a home we could move into and call our own.

❖ **Achievable**: We both had jobs and knew we could buy the home we wanted to if we saved money every week.

❖ **Relevant**: Having a home to raise a family in was essential to both of us. We didn't want to rent; we wanted security, a place that would be our family anchor.

❖ **Time-bound**: We planned to have the home built in two years, not an unspecified time in the future.

We saved money by not going out every week to eat. We used coupons for grocery shopping. I denied my obsession for shoes and purses. We went to Blockbuster Video instead of going out to movies. I formed a side business- A Classy Affair- which was a wedding planning business. I was able to earn and save $6,000. This meant I had to give up many of my evenings and weekends. We made sacrifices and were able to see our savings grow.

In our marriage, we defined our roles and responsibilities. For instance, he does the grocery shopping, which is fantastic, because I hate grocery shopping. I suppose this grew from the marathon shopping sessions I had with my mother. One of my mother's joys was taking her time going up and down every aisle. She would look at labels and talk to people along the way. This seemed this was her time to socialize. For me, it was torture, because I just wanted to hurry up and get home. So, when my husband offered to be in charge of buying the groceries, there was no hesitation on my part. The downside was that he was a health nut, and I believed that cookies were a food group. Since he does the shopping, we eat healthy, and I have to wait until Girl Scout cookie season.

We contract and agree on finances, how we raise our children, and how we build our businesses. We make them formal by writing them down. When things have become problematic, or we're getting off track, we can use these contracts to remind each other what we promised. Our 25 years of marriage haven't always been a bed of roses. But at least we've reduced some of the problems that could have arisen because we have a plan. We run our home like a business.

Be Flexible

Sometimes goal planning and contracts can go too far and be too stringent. Plans can change, and our focus can shift. When we're presented with new information, we may want to pivot away from our old goals and pursue new ones. Or we might want to slightly alter our course and expectations with the new goals we create for ourselves. It takes a certain amount of flexibility to make those shifts when they are warranted.

If you are too rigid, this can cause you stress, which can affect your mental, emotional, and even physical wellbeing. Like me, my children have taken on the tradition of planning (I believe it was imprinted in their DNA). But sometimes they can become too rigid in their thinking, and I have to tell them to relax. Life is going to happen, and you have to keep your eye on the big picture.

If you've ever entered a maze, you know that the way to the exit isn't a straight line. There are turns and dead ends. Sometimes you must backtrack and take a new direction, only to find another dead end. You must make those adjustments and U-turns with the understanding that you will eventually reach your destination.

When you think of your life, you can see it as a straight line behind you. One event leads to another. That's what people refer to as 20/20 hindsight. We can see the pathway we have walked. In front of us is this superhighway with ramps, exits, bridges, and one-way streets with multiple intersections. We might see the emerald city in the distance, but there are so many different pathways to get there. Some are fast, clear highways. Others have obstacles that may require us to take a detour. Along the way, there are also shiny things that we may choose to look at, and that will require us to exit our path.

Can you imagine traveling through your city using a steering wheel that didn't turn? Yet when we're rigid in the pursuit of our goals, we're in for a scary ride.

Mapping Your Businesses Future

ARDX has grown during periods when other companies have crumbled. I attribute this to our having *goals*. We knew where we wanted to be, and we had a plan to execute.

Think of a business as a large ship. The captain has the map with the destination in mind. On the map are landforms and markings where there might be a danger. It would be a blessing if the ship had a perfect wind blowing in the direction the vessel needed, all while on calm water, but this isn't a realistic depiction.

There will be storms, and everyone aboard the ship must do their part to assure the ship remains on course and doesn't smash onto the rocks. Everyone knows what they must do, and with a strong captain at the helm, they can weather the storm and make it safely to their destination. If a ship is blown off course after a storm, a good captain can always adjust their direction to get back on the path. They can look into the sky, see the north star, and regain their bearings.

It's all about the ultimate destination. Where "X" marks the spot.

SWOT Analysis

One of the ways we can evaluate and monitor the progress of our goals within the context of an organization is using a SWOT analysis. This allows leaders to monitor and evaluate those things that are helping the organization move toward their goals and remove those things that may be holding them back.

SWOT stands for:

Strengths
Weaknesses
Opportunities
Threats

Take any goal you might have and answer the questions in each of the four quadrants.

Strengths
- ❖ What strengths do the people and processes have within your organization?
- ❖ What factors help you stand above your competition?
- ❖ What do other people (customers and vendors) say are your organization's strengths?
- ❖ What are the unique resources your organization has?
- ❖ How are you standing out in your market?
- ❖ What assets, within your organization, are helping you reach your goals faster?

An essential aspect of strengths is that you consider not only those perspectives of those within your organization, but also those outside of it. You can do this through annual surveys or after a transaction.

Weaknesses

- ❖ What areas of your organization need to improve?
- ❖ What should your organization avoid?
- ❖ What do others, outside the organization, point out as weaknesses in your organization?
- ❖ What is causing you to not reach your goals?

Just like strengths, be sure to receive perspectives internally as well as externally. Sometimes we have a hard time seeing the problems within an organization, while others can see them easily. While it can be unpleasant to face the weaknesses within your company, you must address them. The head in the sand approach rarely works long term.

SWOT not only functions at the corporate level, but it can also work on an individual level. I have people complete a personal SWOT so that from a management perspective, I can see the concept they have of themselves and help them overcome their weaknesses and threats. A threat may be that they live in a different city and they have a nightmare commute. This threat can create stress for them before they even arrive at work.

Another example was a person within my organization who has many strengths. However, her family and personal life are out of control, and this has impacted her ability to continue to work within my company. She didn't share her issues early enough for us to come up with solutions, like taking time off. So, we had very few choices other than her leaving the organization.

People bring their whole selves to work. It's not just the strengths or our ability to do a specific job. Our emotional selves and our personal life can't be separated from our work persona. SWOTs can help create lines of communication that can reduce threats.

Unfortunately, in corporate America, we're taught to be rough and tough. That we're these machines that show up for work, and anything else in our lives has to be set aside. We can't be authentic, transparent, or vulnerable. This is a mistake because it can steer us to a breakdown.

I don't think we should overshare, but when threats begin to overwhelm us, communication and sharing can help us feel supported, and solutions can be found.

Opportunities

❖ What opportunities are there for your organization?

❖ Are you able to spot the opportunities when they're present?

❖ Where are you looking for new opportunities?

❖ What do you do when you spot a new opportunity?

Opportunities can appear in different ways. There can be a change in the market. New technologies can become available. There may be opportunities to interact with a new and broader audience. Or, you might have to look for them. Policies within your market, as well as new regulations, can change the game. The key here is to be ready and have processes in place to take action once you've identified that opportunity. Also, consider your strengths and determine what opportunities they may unlock for you.

Threats

❖ What obstacles are preventing you from achieving your goals?

❖ What things does your competitor do better than you?

❖ Are there aspects within your market and sector that are changing?

- ❖ Are there cash flow and finance issues within your organization?
- ❖ Are there issues that threaten the continued viability of your organization?

Sometimes threats are out of our control. However, you should be aware of them and be prepared. Threats can be like an oncoming hurricane. We know it's coming, but there's nothing we can do to stop it. But with enough warning, we can secure our house and belongings and get to a place of safety.

Social Experiment

In ARDX, during years five through seven, we did a social experiment with our associates in which we discussed their dreams and hopes for advancement and growth. This is a great time to do a SWOT analysis to determine where you are and what challenges you may face.

Our experiment found that 33% of the people that go through this exercise agree on the path and are engaged in the process. Another 33% aren't sure and maybe aren't ready to confront some of the threats and weaknesses they face. Another 33% have such outrageous goals that they aren't attainable.

It could be that they just graduated from college and want to be a VP in a year. It's an excellent opportunity to talk about SMART goals and breaking down what they want to accomplish into those smaller, more attainable goals. Of that 33% that engaged in the process, the majority of them will achieve the position they want.

You can transfer all the skills I'm sharing from entrepreneurship to intrapreneurship. When you are passionate about what you do, and what we're doing in the company aligns with your vision statement, you can become a better employee. If they don't match, then you may ask yourself if you are in the right position or even in the right company. I'm not suggesting you should quit your job tomorrow. But think of ways to align what you do with who you are.

Task Committee

At ARDX, we accrued enough money that we thought about ways we could grow. We invested money into research and development. We decided that we were going to train other companies on insurance documentation issues and implementation. It cost the companies a lot of money to send their employees to the training.

We developed a committee to create an education module that companies could license and use with their employees. A program that would provide them with the same information they could obtain from attending our training sessions.

There was an employee—I'll call her Martha—who was the head of that committee. She really liked this idea and helped create a vision for the project. That vision resulted in new product that we still sell six years after its inception, with over a million dollars in revenue.

Case Study: Nina

Nina comes from a family of five girls. She grew up in an intact family in Memphis, Tennessee. Her mother and father were always providing learning experiences for their daughters. They wanted to help them grow, be prepared, and become independent women one day.

You can never become what you haven't seen. If Nina had never pushed her horizons, her story might have ended there.

In 8th grade, just before the summer break, Nina received a pamphlet from school describing the ELG program. She brought it home and shared it with her parents, and they signed her up, along with two of her sisters, for the sleep-away camp that summer.

Even though Nina came from an area full of poverty, she felt she lived in a home full of love and was grateful for what her family gave her. She witnessed and was empathetic to her extended family and classmates, all of whom were impacted by poverty and came from homes void of the kind of love and support that she experienced.

Transitioning from middle school to high school can be a stressful time for girls. When she entered the program, Nina was shy and introverted. She had some trust issues and had learned that not everyone had her best intentions at heart, and she was a little wary of new relationships.

When she arrived, she was a bit overwhelmed and wasn't sure if this was the program for her. Over the week, she learned to trust other people, and she began to grow. She had never really thought about being an entrepreneur and was excited about the prospect. She was meeting powerful, successful women who were entrepreneurs, and they started to inspire her.

She was invited at the end of her freshman year to attend the program in Washington, DC. As she boarded the plane, it became clear that she was stepping into a new world of possibilities. She was becoming an entrepreneur and had clarity about her future for the first time. She was getting a taste of what it was going to be like to go to college, and she was excited.

Nina was involved in many activities and found that transitioning from one activity to the next required a wardrobe change. From this experience, she created a clothing line, Nina Shavon, with convertible multi-use clothes. She began with a pair of yoga pants used for working out that can quickly be converted into a pencil skirt.

Her use of Seed #2 has been essential for her success. She realized she needed to get organized and write things down to make sure she accomplished the goals she had set for herself. For instance, she has a goal of creating two new pieces a week for her clothing line, and she is working on expanding her social network so she can sell three products online per month.

When Our Goals Don't Work Out

There are times when we need to take that eraser and create new goals. Sometimes we need to evaluate (SWOT) whether it is the goal that needs an overhaul or whether it is the people trying to achieve them.

I don't compromise on my goals because others are uncomfortable with my choices. Nor do I give up when I feel resistance. Not everyone understands my vision, and that is just fine. They don't believe in my vision, and the vision doesn't exist in their hearts. At these times, I must be honest with myself, and have an honest conversation with them. I don't need a million people around me to support me. I need a hundred people dedicated and passionate about a shared vision because then I know it can succeed.

When determining whether a goal needs work, I look at those around me to determine if they are the right people to help take my company, my career, or my life to the next level. Sometimes when I see that I'm steering away from my goals and vision, I shuffle my staff to find the right combination of people to move the needle forward.

In my life, I have met a lot of wonderful people who have a lot of strengths. However, they had a hard time connecting to my vision. Because of their own past experiences, it was hard for them to understand my vision because they had never experienced anything like what I was trying to achieve. I was aiming to build Disney World in the middle of an orange grove. I had to find others who could understand what I was trying to achieve so they could help me get there.

It takes faith to believe in your vision. I think that a higher power is helping me see my vision and make it a reality. You can't allow others to say that your goals are impossible. If they aren't feeding your soul, then they are taking away from it. You must have an unshakable faith in yourself and God. Therefore, there is no failure; there is only a shift or pivot. Always keep your eyes on the bigger prize.

Activities: Take Action

We think about all kinds of things throughout the day. If you write down your vision, you are one step closer to success. It doesn't have to be the great American novel. Just write down a few sentences that embody your vision. You can add to it later!

Here are some questions to get you started.

- ❖ I am at my best when...
- ❖ I am at my worst when...
- ❖ What do I absolutely love to do?
- ❖ My natural talents and gifts are:
- ❖ If I had unlimited time and resources, and I knew I couldn't fail, I would...
- ❖ If I could invite three people to dinner, I would ask...

Now put your answers together.

My vision is:

Chapter Four

Speak it and Bring it to Life

Can you imagine a group of over 250,000 people standing and listening to the speech of one man? They came from miles to hear him speak on the steps of the Lincoln Memorial in Washington, DC, on August 28, 1963. So many people were moved by Martin Luther King Jr.'s words, drawn to his power.

"I am not unmindful that some of you have come here out of great trials and tribulations. Some of you have come fresh from narrow jail cells. Some of you have come from areas where your quest for freedom left you battered by the storms of persecution and staggered by the winds of police brutality. You have been the veterans of creative suffering. Continue to work with the faith that unearned suffering is redemptive. Go back to Mississippi, go back to Alabama, go back to South Carolina, go back to Georgia,

go back to Louisiana, go back to the slums and ghettos of our northern cities, knowing that somehow this situation can and will be changed. Let us not wallow in the valley of despair."

Can you imagine speaking and having people from far away come to hear you? Can you imagine speaking words that had the power to shape the world and imprint a moment in history?

There is no real magic in words, other than the meaning we give to them. Letters are merely shapes, words are merely shapes put together, and the spoken word is merely bringing these shapes to life through the sound of our voices. But we cannot deny that words have power.

In the movie (and comic book) *Spiderman*, his aunt says to Peter Parker, the alter-ego of Spiderman, "With great power comes great responsibility."

We have the responsibility not only to use our words but to choose the right words. Martin Luther King Jr. chose his words wisely in order to inspire and uplift the people who listened to him. Words can be used to hurt and even repel others, so we must be careful how we use them, and what our intentions are.

You begin with a vision, "I had a dream..." You write down that vision, as Dr. King did in the form of a speech. Then he spoke the words to the world, and with them, changed the world. He started a movement with his words. That is the power to Speak it and Bring it to Life.

There is a power when we look someone in the eyes and tell them what we intend to accomplish together. This is why people flocked to see Dr. King in person. They wanted to hear him and be in his presence. It's the same thing when we go to live events; the energy is all around us.

Have you ever told a story about an event, and the other person gives you a blank look? You remember the situation as funny, but they don't even crack a grin. What do we usually say in that situation?

"You had to be there."

Being present and speaking to others has a very different effect than sending a memo or an email. When something is important, and you really need someone's attention and cooperation, speaking to them in person can move mountains compared to a short text or email. You can see their expressions and determine whether they are understanding you or not. You leave less to interpretation or guesses of your intent. Communication opens up when we speak our thoughts aloud.

Run Toward the Vision

When you speak to others about your vision, you bring it to life. Those who are aligned with your vision will run toward it, like those 250,000 people in Washington, DC. That was not King's first speech, but it was his most famous. He had spoken to smaller groups all over the United States, and when he decided to speak on the steps of the Lincoln Memorial, people rallied to see him. Even those who had never seen him before were energized and inspired by his message, and so they did what it took to be there that day to hear his words.

When we speak our vision, those who are aligned to our message will lean in closer. This will allow you to attract the right people to your organization. If you don't verbalize it, you won't be able to attract the right people.

Once I became the leader of an organization, the power dynamic shifted, and I needed to be held accountable. By speaking my vision and goals to everyone around me, I put in place a strong accountability practice. I learned this lesson from my past, and I made sure that I spoke annually to my associates. I let them know my mission and the mission of ARDX.

Not only does speaking your vision attract the right people, but it also makes you accountable to those words. When we communicate our vision, we make a pact. We promise others that our words have depth, meaning, and value. **If you speak, it will happen.** That's why the previous seed (Put Pen to Paper) is so important. You must organize your thoughts and make sure that your goals are achievable before announcing them to the world. Remember, words have power. The wrong words or making empty promises could damage your reputation and that of your business. Use the right words, and you can inspire growth and loyalty.

When we speak our vision, it is important that we have thought it through and are committing to making our words a reality. When you speak the vision, you own the vision.

Using Your Voice to Be Heard

Speaking up helps your voice sing over a crowd. Can you imagine if Dr. King spoke softly and did not use a microphone? Who would have heard his message? He stood straight with pride and spoke proudly and loudly. His confidence in what he was speaking about uplifted his worlds around the world when it was televised. He was not afraid to speak the truth, and he believed, as I do, "The truth shall set you free!"

My children have learned to speak up for their ideas, too. My husband and I parent differently; I want to hear their thoughts, and he is more about the logistics (how someone is going to get from point A to point B). When my oldest child was in kindergarten, she had a project about Maine, a place she had never been to. She wanted to see the state for herself. She used her voice and told us what she wanted.

My husband thought it was a crazy idea, but I thought it was a great one! The following summer after she completed her project, we visited Maine as a reward. It would never have happened if she had not spoken up.

Since then, we have encouraged our children to let us know where they would like to visit each summer. We have been to some fantastic places, like Greece and Costa Rica. They have learned the power of speaking up; they took their vision and created a reality. Because they spoke up, they were heard, and together we could find a way to accomplish their dream of visiting a new place.

Because I encouraged my children to use their voice, they don't shy away from telling us what is on their minds, especially if it something important to them. My oldest daughter was convinced from an early age that she was going to go to college. She asked me for books that compared different college programs so that she could study them. She decided in the 6th grade that she was going to go to NYU to study drama. She contacted the school and made arrangements to tour the campus during her spring break.

When she arrived, the school was a little shocked. She was only a sixth grader. She remained convinced that this was the school and the program she would attend. As most teens do, in her quest for independence, she made some bad choices that were uncharacteristic for her. I reminded her that if she continued to mess up, it could impact her ability to go to NYU. This struck a nerve with her.

The next morning, she stomped into my room and said that nothing was going to stop her from going to NYU. She was pretty dramatic. She declared that she was going to be successful and that I wasn't going to ruin her dream. After she stomped out, my husband was upset with her level of disrespect. I instead was impressed with her ability to state her purpose and stick to her goals, even when she had a setback. In the end, she did go to college and became successful, though it wasn't NYU and she did she not major in drama. Although her focus changed, her overall goals didn't. She had not been afraid to speak up and be heard.

The Stage

Through ELG, I'm trying to awaken a generation of girls to learn to use their voices. I tell them to be careful because you need to choose what you are going to use your voice for. If it's misused or used for the wrong purpose, then your voice will begin not to matter.

It can be hard for young girls and even women to find their voice. For generations, children were "seen and not heard." We didn't have a voice and were not encouraged to share our thoughts, dreams, and visions. In ELG, we encourage the girls to speak their truth. Speak it out into the world. Let the world know your intention. Your voice matters. Your vision matters. Your words matter. I encourage parents of our Boss Girls that the greatest gift they can give their children is their ear. Listen to them. Encourage them to speak and to share. It builds confidence and character and will serve them well later in life.

When the girls finally step out on the stage at the end of the week, they stand before an audience and speak their vision of the business of tomorrow. They bring their ideas to life through their voice to everyone listening.

ELG Elevator Pitch

Sometimes it is not a large group of people we are talking to; sometimes it can be a single person we meet on the elevator. In the time it takes for the elevator door to close until it opens again, we might have the opportunity of a lifetime. We can stand and chose to remain silent, or we can seize the opportunity by finding our voice.

In ELG, we work with the girls on their elevator pitch. It's a short statement, to the point, and something they can bring to mind instantly. It's that opportunity to speak about what they *do* and what they *intend to do* in just a few minutes.

We tell the girls that they are going to ride an elevator for three floors. While they are riding, Oprah steps onto the elevator. They only have a few minutes to pitch who they are, and their idea, before the door opens. We ask them if they intend to gawk at her, or would they take the opportunity to pitch to her? Would they be clear, to the point, and attract her to their ideas?

Once, at a VIP event, I had the opportunity to meet Michelle Obama. It was an event I will never forget. President Obama took the stage, and my friend and I were three rows from the front. After he spoke, we were able to meet the First Lady. When it was my turn, I shook her hand and said,

"Hello, I love your initiatives with girls around the world. I have just finished my Ph.D. and have created a program to help girls..." and I launched into what ELG was all about. I saw other people were half-fainting when they met her, but I was ready and on a mission to tell her about ELG. I used my voice to own that moment. I had captured her attention! Always be ready.

Networking at events is another opportunity to use your voice and share your vision. I used to hate networking. It was a necessary burden that felt awkward and I tried to avoid it. That was until I figured out the secret to networking: be on a mission to learn about other people. I found that people love to talk about themselves. I developed a list of standard questions in my head to get them started. I listen intently and allow them to speak. I learn so much about the other person that I can begin to make connections to the things we have in common. I can then take the opportunity to share my vision, values, and ideas with the other person at a level where we can both align with one another.

Challenging Tasks

When I was first hired to work in the area of Medicare, before developing ARDX, I knew very little about it. I was placed in a department that was a slowly sinking ship, although they didn't tell me that at the time. I had to get the department into shape or my tenure was going to be short. My job required me to take a crash course on Medicare and then go on the road to speak to others around the country. I had to figure out a way to make Medicare and its claims attractive to people. No small feat. I was Peter Parker, given Spiderman powers, and it was a huge responsibility.

I was speaking to CEOs and CFOs of insurance companies, and my job was to connect the dots for them and to make it feel less threatening. When I have a new goal and task before me, I immerse myself in the content. I try to learn as much as I can and then put my spin on it. This way, I can forge a path for myself and take ownership. Because I was gaining in knowledge, my confidence grew, and I increased my credibility. People listened to me and saw me as an expert and a partner. Through hard work, continued learning, and speaking to others about what I had learned, I created a following and a reputation.

I became the friendly neighborhood Medicare expert. This realization occurred when my grandmother, my mother, and daughter were joining me on one of my business trips in NYC. Two women entered the train we were on, came over, and said, "Hey, you're the Risk Adjustment Lady." This was my moniker. The two women had been in my training session and had a number of follow-up questions. My family looked on with amazement that I had been recognized. Granted, I was not talking in front of 250,000 people in Washington, DC, but nevertheless, I was sharing my expertise and was making a significant impact on the companies I was working with.

Case Study: Chanel

Chanel isn't only the Stakeholder Manager for ELG; she is much more. Growing up, Chanel looked for happiness in all her relationships and also in her career. This was important to her, and it's the passion that leads her life.

Chanel's family believed that she should go into the medical field in college because that was a reliable way to make money. It wasn't something she was initially passionate about, but she wanted to make her family proud. She enrolled in a physical therapy program, but what she truly wanted to do was go into marketing.

By the end of her sophomore year, she knew she had to make a change. The following summer, she did an internship with ELG working as the Summer Experience Counselor Lead. Her job was to help recruit counselors. A large part of that internship was marketing. After this experience, she knew what she wanted to do and began taking classes in business and marketing.

After graduation, she tried to get a job in pharmaceutical sales or in a company where she could use her new skills. She landed a job at ELG as the Stakeholder Manager. She coordinated and helped recruit Girl Bosses, lined up volunteers, and worked with ELG's Title One partners in schools.

She loved her job, but something was missing. Because she was passionate about social media, she wanted to use her skills in this type of work. Chanel shared with us that when she was in her junior year of college and was shifting into the business school, she told her friend that she'd like a job in social media marketing, speaking her intention out loud.

As she began working at ELG, she noticed we had a gap in social media marketing. She once again spoke her intention, telling me she wanted to do this type of work at ELG. We allowed her to take that on, and now she has added that component to her position as Stakeholder Manager.

We asked her if it was harder to sell her idea (to be a social media manager) to ELG or to convince herself? She replied that it was harder and necessary to convince herself first that she could do it. She had no formal education in the area of marketing, but she knew in her heart she wanted to do it. She spoke about her dream aloud and made it a reality.

Chanel wants to leave a legacy for her future daughter. She wants to be proud of what she has accomplished. She's discovered that if life does not have a pathway already built for you to pursue your passion, you have to create that pathway yourself.

Activities: Take Action

Imagine you are on the dream trip of a lifetime: a safari in Africa. Would you leave unprepared? Or would you plan that trip? You would pack the right clothes, bug spray and sunscreen, and of course, have a camera ready to take pictures. You would hold that camera in your lap the whole time, prepared to catch anything of value you saw on that journey. It could take months of preparation!

Preparing an elevator speech takes planning as well. It should be concise, to the point, and you must be ready to share it on a moment's notice. Getting it right takes time and a little practice, but when the time comes, you will be prepared.

How can you capture someone's attention is just one minute? Imagine it is a person who can make your dreams come true—someone like Oprah. Below is a simple template you can follow. Spend time working on the answers and write them down. Put your pitch on an index card and practice it in front of a mirror. Then try it out with your friends and family. You've got this!

1. Define Who You Are: Write one sentence about who you are.

2. Describe What You Do: Using your mission statement as a guide, write one to two sentences about what your skills and accomplishments are.

3. State Your Goal: Identify and define what you're passionate about and what you're striving toward in life.

4. Give your "Why": State what makes you unique and why your audience should invest their interest in you.

Activities:
Take Action

Define
Who You Are:
Write one sentence about who you are.

Describe
What You Do:
Using your mission statement as a guide, write one to two sentences about what your skills and accomplishments are.

State
Your Goal:
Identify and define what you're passionate about and what you're striving toward in life.

Give your
"Why":
State what makes you unique and why your audience should invest their interest in you.

Activities:
Take Action

Chapter Five

Inhale and Exhale

IN MY TEENS, I remember playing the piccolo in the cherry blossom parade in Washington, DC. It is a commemoration of the approximately three thousand cherry trees gifted from the Mayor of Tokyo to the United States in 1912. It is also a tribute to the cherry blossom festivals in Japan. I wasn't playing in a high school band, as you might think. I was playing instead in a Buddhist organization, the Young Women's Kotekitai. We were marching for world peace. We were involved in the band because my mother was Buddhist and was raising me in that philosophy (she dedicated herself to Nichiren Shōshū Buddhism when she was in college). Some of my fondest bonding times with my mother were through Buddhism.

Every time I'm in Washington, DC, and see the cherry blossoms, I'm reminded of marching in that eclectic band of others while playing "Impossible Dream" from the show *Man of La Mancha*. Because I too have dreamed an impossible dream and made it a reality in my life.

I remember all the different people involved in the march—different socioeconomic backgrounds, different races, and different ages. It was a melting pot of people. My mother was the leader of the youth division, and we traveled to some fun places like Hawaii. Being a part of these trips was an eye-opening experience. Being a part of Buddhism gave me a new and unique perspective. It taught me to accept all people regardless of what they believe or where they come from, which allows them to be who they are without judgment.

Inhaling and Exhaling

Seeing those cherry trees remind me of the very special relationship we have with them. We need oxygen to live. Every time we inhale, we bring life-giving oxygen into our lungs, and that oxygen is transported all around our bodies, helping us function, and think, and move. Without that life-giving air, we cannot exist.

When we exhale, we release toxins from our body. When our body uses the oxygen in cells and organs, it produces carbon dioxide (CO_2). That CO_2 must be released from our bodies, and it is expelled through our lungs. In with the good, out with the bad.

God created trees not only for their beauty, but also to be homes for creatures and to produce fruit for nourishment. One of the most important functions of trees, at least to us, is that they produce oxygen. They inhale our CO_2, which is essential for photosynthesis, and they exhale oxygen. (Not exactly like we do, because they don't have lungs, but I am sure you get the idea.)

We need trees and they need us.

In our businesses we also inhale and exhale. Instead of oxygen, it is people who breathe life into our vision. When we create, write, and speak our vision, we attract those who are aligned with us. They bring life to our vision and help us bring it into reality. Sometimes we need to exhale and release those who are not aligned, as they can pull us away from our goals.

The Tree of Our Life

This is your vision, and you need to stay connected to the people who will cheer you on and lift you up! When things get tense, it is time to inhale, and bring the team together to provide support and solutions. These are the people who have your back and want the vision to succeed as much as you do.

I inhale every day because I know that God has my back. My faith leads me. I prepare myself every day to face any challenges and possible adversity. Before I go into the office, I sit in my car and pray:

"If you can use anything, Lord, use me.
If you can use anything, Lord, use me.
Take my hands, Lord, touch my feet.
Touch my heart, Lord, speak through me."

Where I show up, He shows up. My intention is to be a walking billboard of possibilities. This helps to hold myself accountable for how I show up for other people. The other part of that prayer is the gift of discernment to recognize people who feed my soul and those who don't.

One of the challenges most of us face is that we try to force people to be what we want them to be, rather than accepting them for who they are. We must put the people in the right buckets in our lives.

I don't believe in any mistakes. People are placed in our lives for a reason. Think of your life and those you meet as parts of a tree.

Trunk and Roots. These people are our rocks, our foundations. No matter what wind or storm blows against our tree, they will hold it steady and strong. These are the people who make up the base of the tree and are with us long term. When we inhale, these are the people we connect with and rely on. Without a firm trunk and roots, a tree can fall. Our roots are also where we draw our nourishment from; these feed our lives, our souls, and our vision.

Branches. Every part of a tree has a purpose. A tree without branches would just be a stick in the ground. We want growth. Those people who are the branches are there for a shorter amount of time. They will provide us what we need, and then they break from us. This is a natural cycle, and when they are ready to go, we must let them. Sometimes a person can start as a branch, but they may grow larger in our lives and become part of the trunk.

Buds. I love seeing cherry blossoms. They are beautiful and bring joy to those who behold them. Those blossoms start off as buds on a tree, full of potential and provide a means to grow new seeds (new opportunities). Those buds may bloom into something grander and more beautiful. They have a season and a time in our lives, and then they pass or float away to grow into a new tree.

Leaves. As the name suggests, these people come and leave quickly in our lives. These are people who might be brought into a project, or they may just be a person we meet at a networking event and they make another connection to someone they know. These folks come and go in our lives and serve a purpose, no matter how small or brief. They bring life for a short period of time, and when we exhale, the wind blows them to their next destination. Sometimes as leaders we want leaves to be a trunk or root, but they aren't. Leaves are meant to be full and supportive of the health and growth of the tree for a time, and then they're expected to fall away.

Who are the trunks and roots in your life? The branches? The budding blossoms or leaves? Knowing where a person fits within your life, or within your organization, helps you know whether you can inhale with them, or exhale and let them go when the time is right.

Pink Cadillac Journey

I've been a girl-preneur all my life. I've always been the girl packing and trying to sell things. I sold Mary Kay just after college. I remember singing at the end of a meeting the Mary Kay version of the song, "I have the joy, joy, joy, down in my heart..." I learned so much from my Mary Kay experience. I was surrounded by women who lifted me as I moved up through the company. There was a clear vision within Mary Kay, and so within three weeks of starting, I was able to assemble a team around that vision. These were women like me whom I could inhale with. We shared a high level of enthusiasm that was contagious.

Gloria Mayfield Banks is an Elite Executive National Sales Director for Mary Kay, Inc., and my heroine. I watched her videos and heard her talk live; she was very influential to me. I was impressed that she had an MBA from Harvard Business School. Through her, I learned a lot about business. She embodied the principles of Mary Kay: God, family, and career. In that specific order. As I think back now on my time with Mary Kay, it was less about the lipstick and more about their philosophy and business principles. Her principles allowed me to exhale and to move up the ladder within Mary Kay. I use some of those same principles today.

While we are not close, her presence in my life exists in my roots, as her principles help me when times get tough.

My Dorothy Moment

When I became pregnant with my daughter, I remember walking around the neighborhood and realizing there were no magazines for children of color. There wasn't a magazine that talked about specific hair needs and skin regimens. I remember the feeling when I went to a school where no one looked like me. I felt alone and like an outsider. I didn't want my daughter to feel that way.

I had another "Dorothy from Kansas" moment, like when Dorothy realizes that her goals and dreams were with her the whole time. All she needed to do was click her heels to return home. When she did, she brought back all the memories and lessons from her adventures in Oz. My ability to help girls was my power. I needed to inhale. So, I had the audacity to come up with a magazine for children of color.

My husband heard my vision and was behind me. Without him, the idea would have died before it had a chance to breathe. Our *Pride & Joy for African American Parenting Magazine* became a reality. We had a distribution of 25,000 copies every other month. We spared no expense. It was quite the production. We had a team of freelance writers, photographers, and editors. We also had sponsors for the magazine, and it was a joyful experience. Unfortunately, when 9/11 occurred, people became scared, and all our sponsorship dollars went away.

Finding My Roots and Trunk

Having people around me who share my vision is essential. I am particularly grateful for the women who have stuck by my side. One of my best friends, Charmaine, has been with me since my first day of college. She has always been there to support me and jump into ventures with me. She breathes light into my life.

When I started ARDX, it was a significant strain on my family and my marriage. My life was on shaky ground. Charmaine had a great job at Lockheed Martin in Northern Virginia at the time. She didn't want to see me fail, so she quit her job, moved close to me, and took over the duties of running the office. Charmaine helped with picking up my kids when we couldn't. She took the kids for a weekend so that my husband and I could go on a date or have a weekend to ourselves to help our relationship. She did whatever she could do to help because she believed in me and my vision.

Laurie has been my assistant for many years. When I said I wanted to pursue my Ph.D., she didn't tell me it was impossible. She did the research and found the program that checked off all the boxes for what I needed. She made sure I was able to go to school, and she put systems in place at the office to help while I traveled. She shared my load of work, and I was able to pursue my dream.

I've surrounded myself with a tribe that shares common values, vision, and are unconditionally supportive. None of what I've built would have been possible without the team of people I work with. They are positive, constructive, and always ready to serve in any capacity needed.

Case Study: Monica

A woman who continues to breathe life into me personally, professional and spiritually is Monica. She is the Vice President of Business and Government Operations for the Verizon Business Group. She is also the current Vice Chair of ELG. If I get an idea in the middle of the night, she will always answer my call. She has twins, a husband,

and a high-level position at Verizon, but she has always been there for me when I needed her. She believes in the potential of my visions and acts as a sounding board. She will ask questions and hold me accountable for my ideas. She supports me unconditionally. She is on the board of directors for ELG and is highly active, and no matter how crazy her schedule is, she always makes sure she is at our board meetings.

Relationships are essential to Monica, and she does not take them lightly. She is cautious about who she terms "friend," though this wasn't always the case. Monica grew up with a single mom who worked multiple jobs to try to make ends meet. When Monica looks at her position now, overseeing 16 billion dollars, and where she came from, she states that relationships were the key. Not just any relationship, but the right ones.

She had people who invested in her—mentors and sponsors. They gave her support and guidance and taught her to think differently about life and money, which helped her climb the success ladder quickly.

When she was young, she invested in all types of relationships, with little regard for how people fit in her life and even how she fit into theirs. As she has matured, she has seen the value of investing in the *right* relationships—her core friends. They must support her, uplift her, and be real with her. They must be transparent, honest, and loyal. It's great to have a cheerleader, but it's more important for someone to be honest with you.

There are people outside her core network of friends who have had an impact and are very dear to her. They are not lifelong friends, but they helped her grow and came into her life when she needed them. It's critical to know what role people play in your life and who are the ones you should invest in.

Monica feels very blessed to be on the board of ELG. She sees how the girls we serve learn the importance of good relationships early. They can take in what she learned through experience, though not all of it was pleasant. The board is still young, and everyone is still feeling one another out. Although members of the board come from diverse backgrounds, they are united and passionate about the girls they are serving. As time goes by, relationships between this diverse group continue to deepen and grow.

Board of Advisors

By the 10th year of ARDX, I was ready to expand my vision, so I created a Board of Advisors.

The purpose of the board was to find ways to grow and develop our business. I was careful about who I chose for that board. I needed branches and buds. I needed people who shared my vision to help me to get to the next step.

I invited a corporate executive from a communications company to be the chair because of their experience with larger organizations. I included an HR person too because our company was growing so fast, I was overwhelmed with personnel and hiring issues. I also invited the bishop from a large megachurch because he was a business genius. He could connect scripture seamlessly with people's lives. He could hold me accountable and remind me of how my company had started from humble beginnings with a spiritual purpose. He could teach me how to be a responsible leader of faith. These people became my tree.

Each member of the board took a part of the company and was tasked with presenting a potential area of expansion (Shark Tank™ style). From there, we came up with a brand new concept: XDRA Advantage. A new company focused on working with commercial entities.

Within two years the group met their intended goal and therefore dismantled. It was like leaves falling from a tree and fertilizing the earth, allowing ARDX to grow and create a new enterprise.

The original board of directors for ELG consisted of ten charter members. They were the roots and trunk of the organization. Seven of those original members have remained. They believed in the vision of ELG before it was even a reality. They shared my ideas and supported me in making it happen. I chose them because of their drive and unique skill sets in finance, law, and programming.

I took this same concept to ELG and in 2019, we organized another Board of Advisors. Their purpose was to help us shift from the local community to a more national perspective as we expanded into 48 states. The Board of Advisors were the branches, but we needed to develop new buds within the organization to help us grow and expand in new areas.

Learn to Let People Go

Sometimes it is time to exhale and let people, and even ideas, go. If they are not serving a greater purpose in our lives, they can fester and cause us heartache and stress. This does not make those people "bad;" it is just means they have served a purpose in life and it is time for them to go.

This philosophy has helped me cope and appreciate people more, no matter how they present themselves in my life. I've understood that people are who they are, and I've learned to accept that. For many years, I waited for the phone call from my mother in which she had transformed from the provider to the nurturer. Once I shifted my thinking, I learned to appreciate and love her for the role she has played and will continue to play in my life. I've learned so much from her. I've accepted that she was never meant to be the nurturer, and I love her for the role she played and continues to play in my life. If I held onto that hope, it would have become another unmet expectation in my life. That would have led to sadness and resentment. Today I call her for advice in business, and I understand the positive things she can bring into my life.

Let the haters and naysayers go. Look for the lessons you've learned from your interactions with them. Stop drinking from the poisoned well, and instead choose the well that nourishes you, puts a smile on your face, and sets your soul aflame.

I've mentioned that having the right people in your life is essential. When you have a clear vision and share it with others, you attract those people who will breathe energy into your vision. You want people around you who will support and help you achieve that vision. In that process, you need to leave behind those who would suck the life out of your vision.

Choosing these people isn't an easy vetting process, and it's often full of emotional turbulence. We don't want to be mean or cruel to people. We don't want to burn bridges or hurt people's feelings, either. However, there are times in your personal life and professional life when you must prune the hedges. For a rose to reach its full beauty and potential, leaves and shoots must be pruned. If not, these shoots will pull the plant's energy away from the flowers. People who do not believe in your vision are like those shoots. They drain the energy away from your efforts.

They say that you are the average of the five people you spend the most time with. If the people in your inner circle don't believe in your dreams, soon enough, you won't believe in them, either. If they agree with everything you say without working towards growth, soon your growth will cease as well. It's all about finding the balance of people who are invested in enough in you to give you valuable feedback and help you excel.

Growing a Business

The first year of ARDX was great. We had a tight-knit group of ten, and it felt like everyone was breathing life into the business. Then we grew.

It felt like we were hiring outsiders of the tribe we had formed. I was becoming an entity rather than a person. Although I was the pillar of the organization, I was losing my ability to reach all the players as I once did. I felt like an entity with no heart. That was difficult because people began talking about the "company" and making up stories about me and my decisions.

As a public figure now, people could say whatever they wanted about me. I had to take it on the chin and couldn't retaliate. I had to figure out my new role and understand how my company was evolving. It was a period of darkness.

Because not everyone understood me or what was going on with the company, they prescribed to the MSU University (Make Stuff Up). It was disheartening to me and a very tough time for the company. The negativity spread from person to person.

I concluded that there are people out there who will suck the life out of your vision if you allow it. I was never a person who was part of the negativity. I never had time for the drama, and so I wasn't prepared. There was a lot of praying and a lot of loneliness. There were people who I felt should be defending me but weren't. I couldn't say anything because I was the boss.

I had to dig deep and pray that the vision I saw was meant for me. I had to accept that it was my vision and that others might not share it, and that was okay. However, if they were pulling me and others away from that vision, then I had to let them go.

We set down roots and after thirteen years, we're still here, and the vision is strong. I focused on my goals, stuck to them in the tough times, and celebrated them in the good times. Many leaves have left our tree. I wish them the best and thank them for the lessons they've taught me.

Activities: Take Action

Relationships are a lot like a tree. They need love, care, and nurturing like a tree, and not all parts are created equal.

Think about the people in your life and what part of the tree they are:

- ❖ The leaves are people who are only there for a season and won't be around long term.

❖ The buds are people you are developing relationships with, whom you think could be meaningful once more effort is put into the relationship.

❖ The branches are the people who have been around for some time and will probably stay, but if there is too much adversity, they won't stick around.

❖ The trunk of the tree represents those who have been your support system.

❖ The roots are the people who hold you down no matter what tornadoes, hurricanes, or rain life throws your way.

RELATIONSHIPS

The leaves are people who are only there for a season and are won't be around long-term.

The buds are people you are developing relationships with, that you think could be meaningful once more effort is put into the relationship.

The branches are the people who have been around for some time and will probably stay, but if there is too much adversity, they won't stick around.

The trunk of the tree represents those who have been your support system.

The roots are the people who hold you down no matter what tornadoes, hurricanes, or rain life throws your way.

RELATIONSHIPS

Who are the people that represent your:

leaves

buds

branches

trunk

roots

Chapter Six

Delve Into the Details

I REMEMBER the first time I heard the phrase "The devil is in the details." It was during a large corporate meeting, and the term stuck with me on my long hour and a half commute through D.C. to my home in Maryland. I replayed the phase in my mind for years and never really agreed with the concept. Over time, I have come to think about it differently. Rather than the devil in the details, a true gift of wisdom exists instead.

Making sure you see the details can save you time, money, and heartache. When we moved to Hampton Roads, Virginia, we chose the city and neighborhood where we would make our home based on the test scores of the local schools. We wanted our children to have the experience of going to school with kids in the neighborhood. This had not been possible because they had attended private schools. We still wanted them to have the best education possible, and so the test scores were our metric for choosing our home. The problem is, we did not delve far enough into the details.

After being away from the area for over 15 years and living in the Washington D.C. area, I had grown accustomed to the rich diversity that existed in and permeated the culture. When we returned home, we selected a beautiful community where every lawn was manicured and there was a park on the corner. Our eldest child was only nine and our second child was barely walking, so we imagined we would be in this home for a while. We imagined ourselves living in this community comfortably for many years to come.

It couldn't have been a month after we moved in that we looked outside of our window only to find the largest Confederate flag in our neighbor's yard. I had only seen this on television. I immediately felt fear, panic, and disappointment. This flag would appear off and on for years. Then we learned that, on Friday nights, the four wheelers would gather in the grocery store parking lot, waving Confederate flags.

This mindset began to be a problem in the schools to the point that all the research regarding the test scores didn't matter. The culture made the school experience a nightmare for our eldest daughter, so we left the public-school system and moved to the private school in an adjacent city, closer to our office. We definitely had a vision of what we wanted for our children, but we had not delved into the details enough to check out the community before making a decision to live there. Armed with this information, our next move was a much better cultural fit.

The Overnight Success Myth

There is this myth that you can just look at someone else's success and assume that you can do it, too. Most overnight successes take ten or more years to create. We see the results, but we don't know all the details that brought a person to their shining moment.

When I decided that I wanted to pursue my Ph.D., I had some particular requirements that the program I was going to study in needed to have: a robust research component that included a dissertation and a cohort model that focused on executives. It was particularly important to me to have a peer group with whom I could exchange practical experiences. I was ecstatic to find this program even though it required extensive travel to Oklahoma to attend classes.

Going through the Ph.D. program shifted my business powerfully toward a discipline of data-driven decisions. I make decisions based on strong empirical evidence rather than merely a gut feeling or an emotional choice. This means I ask lots of questions. I'm curious by nature, and therefore I ask a question which leads to many more questions. I keep asking until my curiosity is satisfied. Often, I am less interested in getting the "right" response and more interested in the logic that was applied in the process. I find that I may be able to correct a response, but that is short term. Once I understand the logic, I can better get to the root cause, and therefore create a more lasting change.

Business owners could benefit tremendously by applying a mixed method approach when collecting data. For example, in our organizations we collect quantitative data through surveys including employee satisfaction and customer satisfaction. In addition to metrics that are established regarding service level agreements and quality standards, we also collect qualitative information through focus groups, round tables, and interviews.

One of the most meaningful data collection experiences I had was during my first year in the

Ph.D. program. After reading a journal article, I was inspired to create a President's Advisory Committee. I gathered 12 individuals monthly and discussed the strengths and weaknesses of the company. It was excellent to get their perspectives not only on issues, but also their recommendations regarding solutions. I learned the value of triangulating the data that I collected. In addition to collecting the data from the interviews and focus groups, it was important to refer to the literature to determine theories that explained the findings. The Ph.D. program changed how I made decisions as an entrepreneur and saved significant time and money in the long run. Research is a big part of delving into the details.

While ARDX was formed 13 years ago, I was creating the foundation for this organization almost 30 years ago. My careers in customer service, sales, marketing, training, project management, healthcare consulting, and federal government contracting come into play every day. I gave 100% to all of those roles. I was the first person to arrive and the last person to leave. I was an outstanding employee long before I became an employer. I was determined to become an expert in everything I touched. ARDX was not an overnight success; although we experienced growth at a more rapid pace than most startups, the organization was an extension of my 30 years of experience.

Doing work with the federal government, the largest customer in the nation, is probably the toughest industry to survive. There are complications regarding being in compliance with Federal Acquisition Regulations. I could probably write an entire book on that experience. Regardless of the industry you are in, it is the founder's responsibility to know your business. I would organize this knowledge into three categories. When considering whether you are genuinely prepared to begin building a business, ask if you've dug enough into the details before hanging out your shingle. You need to know:

1.   What you know.
2.   What you know you don't know.
3.   What you don't know you don't know.

Begin with *what you know*. You have the right certifications, you have a certain level of experience, and you have the necessary skills to get the job done.

Once you begin building the business, you will find things *you don't know yet*, but you will work toward building your knowledge. This can mean going to workshops, consulting with other professionals, and formally educating yourself in different ways.

Then there are things *you don't know that you don't know*. These are dangers that we can fall into, and we have no idea they even existed. This is where digging into the details and doing your due diligence is essential. You want to increase the items that you do know and reduce the things you don't see that you don't know.

Because I had become an expert in healthcare management and specifically risk adjustment methodology, and I had spent time in that space when I started my own company, it was relatively seamless. We were profitable from day one. This wasn't luck, but because I spent many years becoming the expert in my business before there was a business.

We live in a society that moves fast, and we want everything instantly. If you order something through a drive-thru speaker, you expect it perfect and bagged by the time you come around the corner and hand them the money. You can go online and buy things with a click of a button and expect to receive it the next day.

Building your expertise isn't instantaneous. Not only does it not occur right away, but you also may make a lot of mistakes and fail a few times before you are ready to be the expert you need to be. It isn't always a straight path—it can be curvy with a steep incline all the way. However, if you want to be successful, you have to take the time and invest the sweat equity on the front end. You can't wallow in the regret of not having been prepared enough on the day your business is closing its doors.

On the flip side, you could suffer from "analysis paralysis." You can spend too much time researching and never move forward. I'm still learning new things even today, so the research and the learning never stops. However, you have to be willing to take the leap when needed and act.

One of the areas that I needed a deeper knowledge of was contracts. Our first contracts were fixed priced contracts. It was critical that we understood the requirements before submitting our proposal because we were locking ourselves into the price we quoted. This was a risky contract type because of the danger of going over budget if we missed a detail such as travel locations or number of participants we could host at a conference. In time, we began winning time and materials contracts, which meant we were being compensated based on the labor and materials for a contract. This made it critical to predict the right number of people and to predict the number of hours each person would need to complete monthly goals.

When managing contracts, paying attention to details was essential. We needed to know how many people we needed to fulfill a contract and what their salaries were going to be so we could set an appropriate budget. These details were essential so that we could bill our customer, the government. We needed to understand the terms of the contracts, as this sometimes meant that we didn't receive funds for 90 days from contract start date. That meant we sometimes had to float payroll until the funds came in and have a firm understanding of cash flow through the company. Not delving into the details could spell disaster when employees are not paid. Thankfully, that was never an issue for us, but I have had experience with many companies who were unable to make payroll.

Location is Important

In addition to contracts, we had to know about the pool of people we were pulling from. We had to have an idea of where we were going to find the right people for the positions we needed to fill.

Since I studied marketing, I understood that for a retail business, place was one of the 4p's of marketing. I also understood that location, location, location mattered for real estate. I underestimated just how much location would impact my ability to create an optimal culture within ARDX.

While I was raised in the Hampton Roads area, I spent my entire professional career in the D.C. metropolitan area. As a young professional, I only knew one speed when it came to my work life, and that was fast. During the first five years of hiring at ARDX, I began to see a trend that, regardless of age, there was an expectation that the workday would end at 4:30 or 5:00 every day. The work that we performed for the government involved extremely high-profile implementations. Our customer depended on us being five steps ahead, and that was not going to be accomplished by 5:00 every day. This demand was challenging the culture of the community from which we were hiring our staff, which resulted in high turnover.

Second, because we were building a business, we had to consider the pool of applicants we were drawing on. Hampton Roads is one of the largest military towns in the United States, and people in the area were used to working in with the defense industry, which was different from the type of staff necessary to work on healthcare contracts. It was hard to find qualified applicants. Therefore, we hired the closest candidate and recognized that we would need to train them. In the early years, we would train for almost a year before we recognized a return on the investment. By the time they were able to fully contribute to the organization, they would be recruited by other organizations. Recognizing a pattern, we implemented a remote staffing strategy. We hired experts regardless of their location and allowed them to work remotely. We saw immediately saw returns on our investment and now only have 10% of the workforce working in the office.

Partnerships Matter

We experienced exponential growth year over year for the first decade of the business, and I attribute that to having partners at the table who were my trusted advisors and made me a smarter business owner. I knew enough to know what I didn't know and I partnered with organizations to fill those gaps.

I absolutely needed a legal team that had a solid understanding of federal government contracting, especially in the professional business services arena. This was more challenging to find than I imagined. I visited over a dozen firms who specialized in government contracting, but they focused on the defense or construction industry. I knew enough to know there would be value to having someone who understood my specific specialty area. There was a premium for this, but I am certain that this provided me with the advice that minimized risk and ultimately saved the company in the long run.

The second partner was an accounting firm that understood cost accounting and tax accounting specifically for the federal government. During those early years, this organization was instrumental in establishing our accounting systems and supporting our compliance efforts until we could build our internal finance department. While the scope of our engagement has shifted, they now perform our audits annually.

The third partner was an HR management consultant who was an attorney. She served as our HR department. I had hired individuals in my capacity as a senior leader in other corporations. What I didn't have experience in was hiring someone on my own dime. I was entirely responsible for the outcomes and staying within the confines of the law. So, for my HR department, I hired an attorney who was an HR specialist who could build my HR department. Making those decisions, in the beginning, has saved me time, money, and grief. They have been and continue to be worth their weight in gold.

I didn't have to know everything they knew. I needed to see that it was in my best interest and that of my company to have specialized professionals like them. Over 13 years, I have learned so much about what they do. They copy me on emails concerning decisions they make about the company. I'm not the expert they are. Still, I know enough now to utilize their skills properly and to make better decisions in their areas of expertise. I could not know all things, so I needed to know enough to invest in hiring strong partners.

I see two common mistakes in business. It is true that, as a startup, you must be scrappy and keep an eye on expenses. There are areas that are worth the investment and that is in professionals who can ensure you don't fall into the traps that exist in business. I would advise businesses to not make the mistake of being scrappy with the areas that create the most risk for survival.

The other mistake business owners and leaders in general make is that we assume that having strong partners means that we are off the hook. Just because we have strong partners around us does not mean we are off the hook. It is important to utilize their expertise and not make assumptions. This means we need to ask questions when something does not make sense. If you are running a business and something happens, it isn't the consultant's head on the chopping block, it's yours. You are responsible for what happens. I'm involved in every nook and cranny of my business because every part of the company is MY business. Besides, we become stronger leaders by asking questions.

What I Didn't Know About ELG

I knew when we were leaving our first stop in Memphis that we were on the brink of creating something more significant. The girls were upset. "You are leaving us, and we won't see you again," they told me.

We didn't want to leave those girls and wanted to be a significant part of their lives, to support their transformation into the girl bosses they were all meant to be. Yes, that meant allowing them to see the opportunities to take their passions and create profit. But more importantly, that meant seeing them become more confident and trust that their voices really mattered. I immediately realized that ELG was moving beyond my dissertation and was here to stay, which necessitated the establishment of a non-profit organization.

My business acumen kicked in and my understanding of data collection and analysis allowed us as an organization to create an incredible and sustainable program. While I serve on several nonprofit boards, they were all well established and in many ways in maintenance mode. I realized that I knew very little about the requirements to establish a 501(c)3.

I went back to the model that had served me well in forming a for-profit organization close to a decade before. I sought out partners who were experienced to close the gap in my understanding in what I didn't know and, more importantly, help determine additional areas that I didn't realize that didn't know.

Based on long-standing relationships in the community, I was able to assemble a phenomenal charter board of directors. I was intentional in seeking out those with legal, financial, operations, marketing, banking, and technology experience. I was careful to ensure some of the members were experienced with a variety of nonprofit board management and leaned on them to make me smarter in that area. Additionally, I spent time with an experienced nonprofit CEO who assisted me with the development of our fundraising plan.

It was this combination of prior business experience and the selection of key resources to participate on the board that allowed ARDX to accelerate through the growth stages that most nonprofits experience. Because the foundation of the program was research based, we had extensive outcome data within the first year of the organization. This allowed us to tell a story in a very compelling way, leading to our ability to build a strong stakeholder base and raise necessary funding.

I remember our first board retreat and the enthusiasm from all those on the board. I was in my element, as it felt like those early days at the ARDX annual meetings. I invited an experienced nonprofit expert to facilitate, and she was blown away at the maturity of the organization, given that we had only been established for one year. That was a major confirmation that we were on the right track.

My takeaway, and the takeaway that I would offer to the reader, is that we have to lean on what we know and continue to grow that knowledge. We can't fear what we don't know, and we must always build relationships with those who have the knowledge and ask for their help. It means that we must be vulnerable and accept that we move faster and more effectively when we build relationships with individuals who are strong where we are weak.

The board rallied around an audacious goal to empower 1,000 girls in 48 states through the power of entrepreneurship by 2020. Yes, this was a daunting task, and honestly, we experienced challenges in that first year determining the strategy to reach this goal.

Recruiting would become a major dependency to reach our mandate. The core team debriefed me regarding a call they had with a potential donor and a question they were asked. "How many Title One schools are you working with?" The team breezed over that question and continued to discuss the other information shared during the call.

My brain latched on to the term Title One schools. Once our meeting was over, I researched the meaning of Title One schools and learned that these are schools that receive federal dollars due to the large concentration of children living in poverty. Bingo, this was our target population. I delved into the details further and found the list of Title One schools in each of our target regions. Eureka, the team created a recruitment plan that was based on working directly with these schools.

That detail made all the difference in our ability to reach our goal. Again, I didn't see the devil in the detail; I saw a tremendous gift that allowed us to create a laser-focused strategy, saving us time and money. I can't give the devil credit for that. We were not able to close the deal with that potential donor where the question regarding Title One schools came about; however, we received significant value by simply having the conversation. A true gift.

Case Study: Danielle

Danielle grew up in a small town in West Virginia. She had a younger brother and stepsiblings when her mother and father each remarried. Few people escaped the small town she was raised in. Most people grew up, had families, and stayed there their entire lives. But not Danielle. From the time she was in first grade, she knew she wanted to go to college. She had figured out the "what," but not the "how."

She found that determination and hard work were essential components to go to college, so she concentrated on her schoolwork. She needed more information about how she could go to college and found the answers in libraries and through her school counselor. Her greatest ally and source of information was Upward Bound™. This is an organization that helps kids learn life skills and how to focus their lives on success for the future. The counselors in Upward Bound™ filled in the gaps of what Danielle "didn't know" and what she "didn't know she didn't know."

The encouragement and knowledge she received made Danielle the first person in her immediate family to go to college. She began attending the University of West Virginia.

Danielle met her husband in high school, and they were committed to supporting one another.

Her husband was in the military and was stationed in Hawaii. She transferred schools to be with him. People from her hometown didn't believe she would finish, when in fact, she wasn't only in college but had left the state to be with the person she loved on a beautiful island. She proved the naysayers wrong and graduated early with the honor of being summa cum laude. Her husband was then transferred back to Virginia. Once again, she followed him and went back to school to receive her master's degree. Even though circumstances had changed, she was committed to her vision of success.

Danielle found a job opening on LinkedIn for ARDX and began working part time as a research assistant. She wanted a permanent position and learned that there was an opening at ELG. As ELG got off the ground, Danielle became interested in working for that company. Upward Bound had helped her as a youth, and ELG would be a perfect way to help girls just like her. Again, she knew the "what" but not the "how." She asked me questions about what I was looking for in a candidate, and she made sure she was prepared.

Danielle's delving into the details paid off, and she was offered a permanent position. She became ELG's data manager and can now tell our story through numbers. She has had the opportunity to meet the girls in person during the camps, and it has been a life-changer for both her and the girls she serves. She knows from experience how being supported and mentored is essential, not only for the knowledge it brings, but also because it helps the participants build their confidence. Once someone believes in themselves, then anything is possible.

Danielle feels strongly that delving into the details should come before planning. When you begin digging into a project, your goals may change. It is essential to know what the big picture is before any significant planning begins. Just one step can alter the trajectory of the whole project.

Activities: Take Action

Dreaming is fun, but you also have to dig in and figure out how to effectively do what you envision. Take time to research individuals or companies doing similar things to those you are interested in and figure out how to fit into the marketplace.

- ❖ How is your idea different?
- ❖ How will you market your ideas?
- ❖ Is there funding available?
- ❖ What do you need to have in place to move forward?

Finding the answers to the big and small questions will ensure your success. The better information you have, the more accurate your planning can be. This means research, and for some people, research can sound intimidating.

Fill out the form below to begin to learn how to research companies. Have fun with it!

How is your idea different?	How will you market your ideas?
Is there funding available?	What do you need to have in place to move forward?

Finding the answers to the big and small questions will ensure your success.

The better information you have, the more accurate your planning can be. This means research, and for some people, research can sound intimidating.

Chapter Seven

Plan Your Success

One of the perks of owning your own business is that you can create policies that benefit the individuals in the organization, and it is a beautiful thing when these policies benefit the business owner also. In the early years of ARDX, one of our policies was that we were closed from December 24 to January 2. Our ARDX associates could enjoy paid time off with their families, and I could enjoy uninterrupted time with mine.

Certainly, I could have taken vacation, but as the owner, even when I was on vacation, I was on call for any issue that arose in the office. That week of silence was bliss! I ran hard and fast all year long ensuring the needs of my internal and external customers were met, and I committed to myself that I would give my family my undivided attention every year at this time. I accomplished this by leaving the country during the holiday break. This reduced the temptation to run into the office to get a few things done while everyone else was off (I knew myself enough to know that temptation existed). As time passed and our portfolio of customers grew, we were no longer able to close our doors for the entire period, but I continued to escape for 10 days and to use this time to focus on my family.

In 2018, we remained in the country for the first time and took a trip to Hawaii. It was an extremely busy year and we waited pretty late to delegate the job of making the travel arrangements. I was counting down and had visions of sun and sand and failed to do two important things: delve into the details and plan accordingly. The night before we were to leave, my stomach sank. We were to have two connecting flights and would be travelling for over 24 hours each way. That meant that when we arrived, we were exhausted and equally as tired when we returned. We lost almost an entire day because we needed to catch up on sleep.

When we finally were able to settle in, I looked out from our room and could see the mountains and volcanoes all around us. I began my annual ritual, reading the *Year of Yes: How to Dance It Out, Stand In the Sun and Be Your Own Person* by Shonda Rhimes. It's a book about how Rhimes challenged herself. As she became more successful and famous, her lifestyle changed. This became her new norm, and because of this, she learned the value of saying "yes," even when it was hard. Many doors could have been closed to her, but people said *yes*. She was inclined to quit before she even tried. What she didn't realize is that she needed to step out of her comfort zone and ask people what she wanted. I love reading that book at the beginning of the year to open my mind and heart to saying "yes" to new possibilities.

One of the things that my husband and I do on these vacations is establish our intentions for the year. In more recent years, we have focused our discussions around 6 Fs: faith, family, finances, fitness, friendships, and fun. This leads to some pretty interesting discussions and helps to ensure that we are on the same page. In some of these areas, we learned that we don't always start in the same book, much less the same page. It is through deep discussions that we determine how we need to plan our alignment so that we, as a family, can move forward.

Faith. We have had many discussions in our family about our belief system, especially what we demonstrate and require of our kids. What is too much? How are we being spiritually fed and how are we feeding? This has sometimes moved us to trying new churches and trying new things at home. One thing that we have come to find meaningful is, once a month, having home church, and no, I don't mean streaming. We actually take on roles at home. Someone selects the scripture and teaches us from scripture. Someone selects a praise song, someone selects a worship song, and someone leads us in prayer. This has been an awesome time of sharing with the kids and watching them engage has really been priceless. Yes, God meets us right where we are in those moments. I find that when our faith is off track, we are off to a shaky year.

Family. As the three children began to have their own social and extra-curricular calendars, it became very easy to just become Uber drivers. We are serious about making plans to build our family up, and that also means building each other up as a couple. We are family. We also have discussions about our role in our extended family. We make plans to call and visit our extended family. If we don't plan it, it simply doesn't happen.

Finances. As we matured, our conversations moved from having savings to having a major reserve to building wealth. We intended to impact generations, and that means we must continue to focus on how our money can work for us, building not only the wealth in the business but also our personal net worth. We discuss what investments we will make and what properties we will purchase.

Fitness. This is nothing for my husband; he wakes up thinking about fitness, but for me, there has to be intention. He is my accountability partner, so I tell him what I am interested in achieving for the year, and he helps advise me on strategies that he knows I will stick with. My goals are typically around eating and basic fitness; his is what triathlon he will register for this year. Yes, we are definitely reading from two different books in this category.

Friendships. Both my husband and I enjoy spending time with couples that push us as a couple as well as we recognize the importance of nurturing longstanding relationships as individuals. This is critical to our happiness and showing up as our best selves for one another and our children, so we talk about relationships that we need to strengthen and maintain.

Fun. When you work with your spouse, you can easily bleed home life and work life. We have to be intentional to plan fun. I love when he surprises me with things like taking a ballroom class together. I also know that if we don't call the third Thursday of the month our day, then weeks will become months and months will become a year, and we would have simply existed. I believe we have to plan to have fun or time gets away from us.

Plan Before You Leap

You may be a business owner, you may work in a business, you may be a student, or you may have one of the most challenging jobs in the world, being a stay at home mom or dad, but regardless of your occupation, planning is important for everyone. It is so easy to jump in and get to work, but the magic is in the plan. Plan your dream so that when a window of opportunity presents itself, you are ready to turn that window into a door.

Planning can be tedious. Not everyone enjoys it or is good at it. You have to do it if you want to succeed! You need to look at the *how* and the *why* of each step before you move forward. You can dream about swimming across the ocean, but you have to plan your journey and be physically and emotionally prepared for the trip well in advance.

How will you actually do what you've set out to do? Each step is critical!

Many people want to skip the planning stage. They want to jump from idea to action, and then they trip and fall because they have not spent the time to map out their course.

I believe one of the elements of my successful businesses is my tendency to plan everything. I can remember my bridal shower. We were going around the room in a "get to know the bride" game. Each person would add something they knew about me that others might not. When it was my grandmother's turn, she exclaimed, "Angie loves to plan." That woman knew me well; it is in my blood.

In college, I would write business plans in the computer lab. I knew my husband was the man for me because he would endlessly listen to my elaborate business plans. I would talk about owning a dance school, and it would have four rooms. I didn't realize then how practicing writing these business plans would help me in the future.

This led me to write plans for project management. I began studying the methodologies of project management institutes. I took those principles and not only applied them to the corporate setting but also to all other aspects of my life.

There are five phases in project management: project initiation, project planning, project execution, project monitoring and control, and project closure. I estimate that 80% of project management occurs during the planning stage.

Planning is in my DNA. My grandmother recognized it. My husband experienced it when we were in college together. I used planning in my creation and growth of ARDX. It clearly defined where we wanted to be and the steps we needed to take to get there.

Project Initiation

This is the stage when a project's value and feasibility are worked out. You need to determine whether the project will work and whether it's necessary. This is so important, because if you cannot justify the need for the outcome of the project, then planning ends at this stage.

During this stage, two tools are often used:

- ❖ Feasibility Study. This looks at the goals, the timeline, and the costs of the project. This is a realistic look at resources and whether there are enough to pursue the project further.
- ❖ Business Case. This document looks at the possible benefits of the project. Often these are financial, but there can be other metrics that can be used to measure success.

If the project passes these two evaluations, then it can be assigned to a team to begin the planning stage.

Around the tenth year of ARDX, I was interested in getting external advice on possible growth opportunities, so I formed an advisory board. One of the outcomes from the advisory board was the establishment of a second entity to build another unrelated service. They came up with idea to spell ARDX backwards and XDRA Health Solutions was born. Once we decided that it was a new business we wanted to try, we determined what resources we had and those we needed. The new company was focused on commercial companies, which was quite different from the government contracts we received through ARDX. Our greatest fear was that we would stretch our resources too thin, and it would negatively impact ARDX.

We performed a feasibility study and determined with the right planning that we could not only add the new company, but we could also become profitable quickly. Part of our strategy was certifying individuals for medical coding through the American Association of Professional Coders (AAPC).

Project Planning

Again, this stage takes the most time, and cannot be skipped. There is planning around timelines, budgets, and outcomes. A project plan provides a guide for accessing and locating resources to make the project viable. It also gives you guidance concerning outputs, risk, and acceptance. A project plan communicates the benefits of the project to shareholders and offers directions on how to manage suppliers.

It is at this stage that possible obstacles are identified and solutions for them are worked out. By the end of the project planning stage, all team members know their roles, the scope of the project, and their individual deadlines as well as expected group contributions.

When XDRA added the certification program, we needed to develop timelines and hire instructors to teach the class. In addition, we needed to create the curriculum. Because we took the time to plan, we were able to reach a 99% pass rate.

In the case of XDRA, we decided that we needed outside help, rather than put a strain on our ARDX resources. We needed to hire new leaders for XDRA and get them up to speed.

Project Execution

Once the planning is completed, it's time for action. Don't get caught up in "analysis paralysis." In your plan, decide on a date to begin and when deliverables are due. In the planning stage, it's essential to be specific. In the execution stage, it's imperative to meet expectations and deadlines. Team leaders must allocate the proper resources with the appropriate people at the appropriate time.

Unfortunately, this is where things can fall apart, as they did for XDRA. During the planning phase, the leaders we hired created unrealistic goals, which then generated a problem when it came to executing the plan. As we progressed, we needed to modify our hiring and advertising for positions so that we learned from our mistakes and targeted the person with the skills and experience needed to execute the plan successfully.

Our certification program was not only successful with our deliverables (pass rate), but because we had done planning ahead of time, we were able to create a budget and cost of the program that produced a healthy profit margin.

Project Monitoring and Control

Projects are not catch-and-release. They require a plan for monitoring progress and adjusting activities as needed. Systems must be in place to deal with scope creep, calculating key performance indicators (KPI), and tracking cost and time variations. Having a plan in place keeps a project moving and on track. When there needs to be an adjustment, it's always better to handle it early on than allowing the project to go off course or stall.

This can mean having regular meetings and reports from team leaders. In them, there should be measurable analytics and projections.

At XDRA, we went through a few project leaders, and as I mentioned above, they had created unrealistic goals for their team. We wanted to be sure that XDRA succeeded because it was associated with ARDX and their reputations were entwined. Because we had monitoring and control in place, we were able to make changes in leadership in six months rather than waiting longer, when problems could become major issues. We returned to project planning with each new leader until we got it right.

Project Closure

All great projects must end, and when goals are met, there should be a celebration. Also, the project's completion needs to be announced to critical stakeholders. This allows resources to be allocated to other projects.

Time should be spent analyzing the success and the overall progression of the project. We learn from our mistakes while identifying strengths for further projects. New processes can be created to make more efficient projects in the future and help build stronger teams.

What I often see is people jumping from idea to execution, without allocating enough time for planning. Doing that wastes money and time. People lose morale. Take the time to plan for scope, resources, and timelines. The execution is the result of proper planning, so without it, you are sitting in a car without an engine or a road.

At the end of each year, we do an analysis of the success of XDRA. We look not only at our profits and losses, but also at evaluations of our program and our instructors. We determine whether the programs are still viable and whether we have room for new projects.

XDRA has changed over time, and its original purpose has run its course. Next year, we're going to use XDRA as a training platform to teach other companies how to grow their businesses. We determined that PBO (Performance Based Organizations) are more profitable. PBOs are allowed more flexibility to manage their personnel, procurement, and other services.

I'll be creating workshops and talks for that purpose of shifting towards a training platform. This means we'll start the process from plan initiation once again.

Risk

One of the things that planning does is help you identify risk. You can mitigate and address it before you are in the middle of the execution. Risks that aren't mitigated become issues, and then you may be forced to remediate and start over. It is much better to be in mitigation mode than remediation mode. You need to stop and fix the risk.

Remember that contract I gave to my husband to sign? Our original plan was to have five children and to have each of those children by a certain age. We did have our first child by a specific time, but I was in "career mode." I was in my Master's program.

The day I walked across the stage, I was already expecting my first child.

While the pregnancy was great, the labor, delivery, and recovery were a nightmare. I began to recognize the toll everything was having on me as a new mom. I realized that I would jeopardize both my family and career if I stuck with my plan to have back-to-back children. I couldn't have had the clarity to know that until I had experienced having my first child. I had to do some risk mediation so that I didn't risk my marriage, my career, and everything that was important to me.

We determined that we needed to stabilize before we brought another child into the world. That stabilization took eight years. This also meant that we needed to adjust the number of children we intended to have if we were going to space them out. So instead of having five like we planned, we had three.

Remember in the last chapter we discussed three different types of knowledge? These areas can help us assess risk:

1. What you know
2. What you know you don't know, and most important,
3. What you don't know that you don't know.

Take a moment to absorb that last statement. In the planning stage, you can address the first two issues—what we know and what we don't know.

I would rather be in the position of mitigating possible risks rather than remediating issues. There is no way to mitigate every risk, and in those cases, we have to determine the cost of that risk. If it is small enough, then the risk may be accepting it and mediating it. In some cases, the risk is too large. I don't believe you can run a business without taking some risk; it is just part of being a business owner.

You might know which key people you will need for a project. You might know that there is a hard deadline for completion. You can plan and be ready to execute that plan because of these bits of knowledge.

You might not know how much of a budget you will need for a project. You can set up a committee to find that answer and prepare a report. Or perhaps you are not sure of the scope of a project, so you would need to have a process for determining that.

You should pay close attention to these first two areas before the project begins so you can mitigate issues before they become issues.

The last part of assessing risk is when we don't know what we don't know. This is handled during the monitor and control phase. In my case, I didn't have a clear idea of the time I would need to recover from my first pregnancy until I went through it. I could have asked friends and family what their experiences were like so that I could try to take the right amount of time to recover. However, the information I was using was based on other people's experiences. I didn't know how difficult it was going to be in my own personal experience.

After I had my first child, I reached that project's closure. Then, I was able to take the information I learned from that experience and have a different approach and expectation when my second and third child came. And I might add, my third pregnancy, delivery, and recovery were a dream. Every woman's experience is different and the whole conception and delivery are miracle in themselves. For me, knowing what to expect completely changed my perspective on the experience. That is just how I am wired.

Wheel of Life

When I was in college, I felt like I had all the time in the world to spend with my friends. There was some truth in that. I didn't have the other responsibilities that came with building businesses, being a wife, maintaining a home, and raising children.

As I got older, I realized that time was something I had little control over. I had to be intentional about how I used it. If not, I found myself never having time for the people who mattered the most to me. I wanted to spend time with those who fed my soul. Just like other items on my daily calendar, I had to plug in time for friends and family and hold that time as sacred as a meeting with a client.

I took this one step further and created a pie chart. There are only so many hours in a day. I wanted to determine which items were my top priorities and how much time I tried to allocate for them.

When doing a project within my company, we had to determine how many resources to allocate to get the job done. In my life, I wanted to learn how many hours I needed to assign to all areas of my life to be sure I was healthy and happy. I like to plan my emotions. I know the things that make me happy, and so those are the things that get the most attention.

I started with the top three things that bring joy into my life. They are my faith, family, and finances. If I fail at any of these, I'm not going to feel good about myself.

Then I moved on to the next three things: contributing something positive in the world, my friends, and building a successful company. I then got to my next three and so forth.

After that analysis, I looked at how I was spending my time, and if it was matching up with the most essential things in my life. I put all the items on a pie chart and gave them the percentage of the time I needed to spend on each of those areas.

There are 8,765 hours in a year. I know that every day I must have at least seven hours of sleep a day. I need to allocate a certain amount of time to eating and so forth. Those necessary functions took up a certain percentage of the pie chart.

I then plugged in the other items in order of importance. It was a way to manage my life and my emotional well-being through time and resource management.

Some people believe that money is the most crucial resource. However, if you don't have the correct allocation of time, you cannot make money. If your mind and soul are out of sync, you can't concentrate and make money. Managing how we feed ourselves and our souls helps us to have better outcomes for the year. That is being intentional.

I've done this exercise at different workshops, and I could see several light bulbs going off among the participants. It's incredible how little time we give to the top three things we say feed our soul.

Planning ELG

After I came up with the concept of my dissertation, I needed to plan. I had to determine which cities were the poorest in the US. Then I needed to prepare the logistics of getting into the Title One schools to begin building a list of potential participants for a weeklong camp. There was a lot of planning and coordinating before we ever started our tour.

We created milestones that we needed to reach as we began to execute the first phase and subsequent phases of the project. We broke each goal into smaller milestones so that we had a clear vision of what needed to happen, what resources needed to be allocated, and what ways we could monitor and control the process.

Once we decided that we were going to expand the program, we began to plan the expansion of cities in 2018, 2019, 2020, and beyond. We also came up with plans for communication. It was exciting to have people come on board, but once there, we had to keep them informed and engaged.

We had to spend time on communication, sending out updates, and delivering our message.

Our goal is to have 48 Board of Advisors members to connect to each of our branch cities. They are the face of ELG for their city. Within a couple of months of launching, we were able to get 32 members (and cities) on board. We had to make sure that our communications were clear and consistent across all those cities. Today we meet quarterly through webinars. These sessions are for training and educating the board members and to ensure we have best practices implemented across our branch cities.

We collected feedback from these sessions and kept our lines of communication open. We embraced the responses we were given and saw them as a great gift. Many people don't like feedback, but feedback is the only way I can be sharper, learn, and grow. I count on the input from board members to verify we're giving enough information to participants and that the communication they are receiving from management and from us is clear and consistent.

Steven Covey says in his book *The Seven Habits of Highly Effective People*, "Seek first to understand, then to be understood." He states that it's crucial to create an atmosphere of helpful give-and-take by taking the time to understand issues fully and to give candid and accurate feedback.

This is about planning your communication. When you can listen and understand what another needs and where they are coming from, you can better supply the response that will resonate best with them.

When you plan your communication, you can keep your eye on the prize and not become distracted by others. My goal for ELG is simple: Let's move. I have no hidden agendas. Most days, I'm not reactive to other people's reactions or agendas. My heart is clear—I need everyone to work with me to move one thousand girls across the U.S. from different cities to different destinations. When you plan your communication and have your goal in mind, your emotions will remain stable, and your targets will light up like a beacon to you and others around you. You move forward.

Suppose you were given $86,400. During the day, someone takes $10 from you. Would you throw away the other $86,390 because you lost $10? Ridiculous, right?

There are 86,400 seconds in a day. If someone says something negative and takes ten seconds from your life, would you throw away the rest of the day? Don't let negativity pull you out of your day. Protect your time and manage your emotions.

Case Study: Pam

Pam is an incredibly special person in ELG because she is a mentor. Without mentors and the work they do on an individual and group basis, all the hard work the girls started at their first summer camp with us would be forgotten.

Pam is a successful businesswoman, and a busy one at that. Until a couple of years ago, she and her husband owned a Hickory Farms franchise. She also owns a retail business, Garden Gazebo, which sells garden-related home decor and gifts. In her spare time, Pam sits on the Retail Alliance board, the Hurrah Players board (a family theater), and the Hope House Foundation (an organization that helps adults with developmental disabilities). She is a mother of grown children and a wife. She also enjoys taking dance lessons and performing on stage.

What is the secret to all that she does? Planning. She creates a schedule and sticks to it—even planning her free time. When she was in college, she was able to wait to study until the last minute and cramming. When she stepped into the corporate world, she realized that planning was a better approach. She was able to accomplish more, was accountable to her boss, and was ready to have more time for the things she enjoyed doing.

She brings her skills of planning into her sessions with her ELG mentees. She creates an agenda for each meeting and sends it to the girls ahead of time. This allows them to be prepared. Having an agenda also helps them remain focused during their sessions. She wants the girls to share and explore ideas, but then she uses the agenda to reel them back in.

During the time between sessions, Pam checks in with the girls and can meet with them through video conferencing without having to be with them in person. This helps them remain organized, be accountable, and meet deadlines—all skills the girls will need when running their own businesses. These girls are busy with their lives in school and extracurricular activities. Having an agenda and times they meet in between sessions keeps them focused and moving toward their goals.

Activity: Take Action

Between now and the end of the year, set some goals for yourself to get to where you want to be. Try to come up with a list of twenty goals that you can achieve in the next twelve months.

These will serve as milestones for you to ensure you are on track to reaching your ultimate goals.

For example, if you are starting a baking company, a goal you can set for yourself in the next month is to try three new recipes for desserts and see which ones are the best. Then, in the following month, try three more different recipes. Set goals for your business as well as personal goals, like improving your health.

GOALS

Between now and the end of the year, you want to set some goals for yourself to get to where you want to be. Try to come up with a list of twenty goals that you can achieve in the next twelve months.

These will serve as milestones for you to ensure you are on track to reaching your ultimate goals.

For example, if you are starting a baking company, a goal you set for yourself in the next month is to try three new recipes for desserts and see which ones are the best. Then, in the following month, you want to try three different recipes. You can set goals for your business as well as personal goals, like improving your health.

20
GOALS

GOALS

1. _____
2. _____
3. _____
4. _____
5. _____
6. _____
7. _____
8. _____
9. _____
10. _____
11. _____
12. _____
13. _____
14. _____
15. _____
16. _____
17. _____
18. _____
19. _____
20. _____

Chapter Eight

Reevaluate Your Plan

PEOPLE KNOW NETFLIX as one of the largest and most successful streaming video companies. In fact, they are now producing original movies and series and competing with other networks and movie studios. But that's not how they started.

Netflix was founded in 1997 and was originally a DVD sales and rent-by-mail company. This was during the time consumers were shifting away from video stores like Blockbuster. Netflix understood the landscape was changing even further, as other companies like Hulu were coming onto the scene offering subscription-based online streaming services.

That's when Netflix knew they had to claim this new space, as people were spending more time online and watching DVDs less. They began their streaming service in 2010 and became a mega-billion-dollar company.

Other businesses also joined the scene. Redbox, for example, offered convenient vending machines for DVDs and, eventually, video game rentals. Blockbuster was slow in recalibrating their vision of brick and mortar video rental stores, and hence they no longer exist. They unsuccessfully tried to create their own "blue box" vending machine service, but it was too late.

Many people remember the iconic red envelopes Netflix initially used in their DVD rent-by-mail service. In 2012, Netflix decided to create a new division, DVD.com, to continue the rental service for those clients who didn't want to make the switch to online streaming. Today, they continue to dominate both the old model and the new one they helped pioneer.

Without the vision and flexibility of reevaluation, Netflix could have gone away as Blockbuster did, and no longer exist.

Make a Decision

When we become adults, we no longer make bad choices; we make decisions. We have the wisdom and experience to make a decision and stand by that decision. You made a decision to begin a business. You made a decision to grow that business. You make hiring decisions and firing decisions. When you are the boss, people expect you to make decisions; they expect a leader.

Choices are things that we may or may not want to do. Decisions are things we have to make. There is an important distinction, as decisions can make or break a company. In the case of Netflix, they made a decision to start a streaming service. Blockbuster made a decision to continue with their brick and mortar video stores. Each decision was made by the leaders of those organizations. Netflix soared and is a multibillion-dollar company. Blockbuster is a story we tell our children and grandchildren.

Reevaluating our plan is a decision we all must make. I talked about doing your due diligence before starting a business—a feasibility study. Then, once you were rolling, I talked about monitoring and control. This is the beginning of reevaluating your business. It is at that point that we must a make a decision. Do we head straight, continue the course, and grow organically? We can allow things that we planted to mature and help them grow.

Or, do we turn left or right. Do we make some adjustments. Do we hire new personnel. Do we increase a department's budget. Do we add a new branch (like I did with ELG and XDRA).

Or, do we decide to abandon our efforts? Perhaps our experiment was not a success. We may decide it is time to shut down a department or choose not to renew a contract. These are decisions that leaders are faced with every day. I am here to tell you that it is healthy and normal.

Imagine the mess a rose bush would become if we didn't prune and shape it. There could be so many vines that the blooms could not grow and mature. There could be weeds growing from beneath, trying to choke the vine.

Businesses are like those rose bushes. You must stand before them and make decisions. Do you make cuts, do you water and fertilize? Do you take a cutting and begin a new plant?

That is not to say those decisions are easy ones. We are responsible for them and must own the outcomes. Not all decisions will be popular ones, but that is okay. You are running a company, not a popularity contest. While I value the input and ideas of others, I am the one who has to make the final decision.

Multiple times a day, we're faced with the decision of which path we want to travel—the "happy path" or the "path of resistance." It would be wonderful if the happy path were the best path, but that isn't always the case. Every time we make a decision or send out a communication, we have to decide what is the best path for *that* situation.

Decisions are rarely black and white, and often represent shades of gray. The decision to change course isn't always an easy one. That is why monitoring, control, and planning are so important.

In our minds, we only imagine the "happy path" where people buy everything we're selling, everyone loves us, and everything is flowers and unicorns. How realistic is that?

Vision statements are living documents. They are meant to evolve and shift over time in congruence with the needs of the company. When you learn more and are in a state of evaluation, you can adjust to that changing landscape. I can imagine what the meeting must have been like when Netflix decided to shift its direction toward online video streaming. There must have been visionaries at the table, as well as the right leadership to implement their new ideas.

Being Done is Better than Perfect

As I mentioned in the last chapter, risk is something that companies can either be paralyzed by or ignore and move too quickly. Sometimes you have to move and shift to get a job done. Sometimes a plan seems perfect to begin with, and even though it doesn't seem all the "what if" questions are answered, it's crucial to move forward. It doesn't have to be a perfect plan because perfect doesn't really exist. Being done is better than being perfect.

I learned this lesson when I began working on my dissertation. Before I could begin work on my paper, I had to present my ideas to a committee. That process was more nerve-racking than the defense of my dissertation. I had really big ideas in the beginning. I wanted to collect survey data and do interviews in seven different cities. It would have been a huge undertaking. I might still be working on it.

A friend who went through the process said, "Your concepts are so broad and the data collection is out of control. You know you don't get extra credit for a dissertation. It is pass or fail. Do you know what kind of dissertation is the best kind of dissertation?"

"No."

"The best kind of dissertation is a done dissertation."

She was right. I had wanted this big audacious dissertation and I wanted it to be perfect. I learned that we reach our goals by getting things done chunk by chunk. I had to create a plan that would work and one I felt I could complete by the time graduation rolled around.

I had to make a decision. I had to reevaluate my plan. Because I did, I proudly walked across the stage on schedule.

Reporting

As I mentioned, we have to monitor our progress and performance. It is at these points that we can reevaluate our plan. We can do this weekly, monthly, quarterly or even annually.

When monitoring the progress of a project, reports are extremely important. In our company, we have a process in place where those in ARDX leadership roles submit reports on a weekly basis. These reports speak to what their goals are and what progress they have made. They account for when things get off track, what efforts have been made to get the project back on track, and the effectiveness of those efforts.

We have also instituted operational review meetings where, every other month, leaders within the company present how their departments are doing in meeting their goals. They report situations that need to be addressed and dealt with. These are important for several reasons.

First, they create accountability. Each leader must be prepared to answer questions about the progress toward their assigned goals. They can't hide in their offices and hope no one notices that things are not on track or that they are not meeting their deadlines.

The second reason is that sometimes the problems one department is having are caused by other departments, or their issues are impacting other departments. This is an opportunity for leaders to come together to resolve issues.

Third, as a group, we can brainstorm whether or not the goal and project need to be changed. Since these meetings happen regularly, bigger problems can be remediated quickly and in an organic way.

We need to be agile. We never want to overlook the 99 things that are going well because we are focused on the one issue. This is why emotional control is so important. When things go wrong and we become emotionally distraught, our ability to make rational decisions can be impaired. We may be inclined to play the blame game. It is a game with no rules and in which everyone loses. I try to avoid this by focusing on the process and not the people. When we can remove some of the emotional responses we have, we can focus on the issues before us.

Healthy Body, Healthy Mind

Having a good, healthy body is important to me, but I hate to exercise. When I was in school, if it weren't for the health component in PE, I would have failed. I could get an A in calculus, but I almost didn't pass PE. When I had to go through the Presidential Physical Fitness test, it was torture. I hate sweating. I was as skinny as a willow branch, but that didn't mean I liked to run around a track.

So, of course, I married a fitness guru. Fitness is his life. Our running joke is that when he came to visit, I would wear the cutest workout gear and look like I hit the gym every day. Once we lived in the same town and were married, he realized that was not the norm. Was that bait and switch? I don't think so. Let's just say his visits inspired me. But as I began to have children, my metabolism stopped working like it used to, and my body changed. In response to those changes I wasn't happy about, I created plans to go to the gym, work out, and take control of my body.

I had to figure out what was going wrong. What was happening with me, psychologically, that caused me to fail? I could make outstanding grades in school, I would build successful businesses, so why could I not beat this fitness thing? I had to think about it hard. It was difficult to fathom how I was able to tackle everything else in my life, but this was the one thing I couldn't control and stick to. I put it in my prayer journal because I didn't want fitness to feel like bondage; I wanted to enjoy it. Not just because I wanted to look better, but because I wanted to *feel* better. I needed more energy, and I wanted to be more active with my kids.

To begin with, I had to break the fitness task down into smaller pieces because the bigger goal was too hard for me to tackle all at once. I chose to focus on running. Every morning I got on a treadmill. It was tedious, but I did it anyway. I began to set small milestones. At the beginning of the year, I was running a nineteen-minute mile. By the end of the year, I wanted to be at a twelve-minute mile.

Once I did it for a few months and built my endurance, I began running outside. At the time of writing this book, I'm at a thirteen-minute mile. I have a goal now of running at 5K at the rate of a twelve-minute mile. To my readers who are real runners, this might not seem very fast, but to me, accomplishing this goal is like winning a gold medal.

To get that far, I had to evaluate and analyze what it was I needed to work through. Without going through that process, I was going to set myself up for repeated failure. I noticed that I didn't do well exercising after work, so now I work out in the mornings. When I began to do that, I immediately started feeling better throughout the day.

Reevaluating ELG

When we started ELG, we thought it was a great program, and because there was no cost to the parents, we would have girls falling over themselves wanting to be a part of it. The problem we ran into fell into the category of the things "we didn't know that we didn't know:" the issue of *retention*.

After the girls were in the week-long camp, they were given a mentor to work with and meetings to attend during the school year. What we had not anticipated was how busy these girls were with school obligations and other groups with which they were involved. ELG slipped off their priority list—they just didn't have the time.

We had to change our strategy, specifically our recruitment. We moved our focus to only recruit girls from Title One schools. Part of our strategy was to have a point of contact, a counselor, in each of those schools to help us keep the girls engaged. The difference in retention was like night and day. These counselors became the new program stakeholders.

The other area we had to adjust was our girls-to-mentors ratio. Our first year, our ratio was 5:1. This was too much for our mentors to be able to coordinate. At the end of the program, we sent out surveys, and one of the questions was about the mentor experience. Based on the responses, we shifted to a 3:1 ratio to make sure each of the girls was receiving enough attention from their mentor.

We also figured out that we needed to cap the number of girls to fifteen per city. Because infrastructure was needed to provide a positive and safe space for the girls, a smaller group was much more manageable. That meant working with five mentors per city.

Now that the program has been working for a couple of years, we've realized we needed to add a new component: college prep. Because some of the girls we began working with were seventh graders at the time, now, three years later, they're in high school and preparing for their next steps. Because we strive to see them all the way through lifelong success, we broadened the program to include a college prep program called Seeds of Promise. It was part of our ELG 2.0 initiative. This program allows us to expand the possibilities for our girl bosses, while also keeping them sticky to the organization, thus increasing our retention rates. Like Netflix, we needed to have a vision beyond where we are today to capture a vision of tomorrow.

Our vision for ELG had to be reevaluated. When we began the journey, we had a goal of reaching 1000 girls by 2020. Guess what? By the end of 2019, we realized we had not seen a vision beyond that point, and that is what began our ELG 2.0 initiative. What prompted me to begin thinking further into the future was seeing one of our girls in high school. She was getting ready to graduate high school, and I knew I did not want our connection to end. We had to think about what was next. Our girls are our customers, and we had an obligation to see them through the next phase of their lives and beyond.

Case Study: Anyssa

Because my daughter Anyssa had grown up living the seeds of success and had implemented them successfully in her life, she became the poster child for ELG. I wanted her to be a model and spokesperson for the organization.

She has gone through the process of making decisions and reevaluating her plan. Her vision for her future started early in life, but as she began the process of navigating that vision, she had to make some tough decisions. I am proud to say that her decisions have paid off for her in huge ways. They were her decisions to make. She weighed the data around her, picked a new path, and stayed the course until she completed her journey through college.

Anyssa wanted to have a career like the enigmatic Olivia Pope from *Scandal*, a drama series written and created by Shonda Rhimes. Pope plays a fixer in Washington, D.C., for rich and powerful politicians. Anyssa wanted to be a crisis manager for power players.

Her plan was to double major in journalism and business administration because she felt the combination of these two degrees would give her the necessary skills to achieve her dream. Sometimes we can be stubborn with ourselves and hold onto a vision rather than listening to the data. We follow our wishes rather than seeing the reality in front of us. Because of this, we can lead ourselves down a dead-end road. I can proudly say that Anyssa listened to the data that was in front of her and quickly learned that being agile and having the willingness to pivot would serve her well.

During her freshman year in college, she began her studies in the journalism department while waiting to be accepted into the business school. Her advisors told her that doing the double major would be difficult, and they advised against it. The class requirements for both majors were just too demanding.

In her sophomore year, she was accepted into business school and was able to see that her advisors were right. She had to make a decision. She weighed her options and felt that either degree would allow her to achieve her goals, but that she didn't need both.

A business degree would give her the most comprehensive range of marketable skills. At the time, she was disappointed because she'd already spoken her intentions to friends and family about doing the double major. She had planned everything out, including what organizations she wanted to be a part of at school so that she was immersed as much as possible in both majors.

Anyssa graduated from UNC-Chapel Hill with a degree in business administration. At 21, a graduate, she had the clarity to know she had made the best decision. She learned the importance of reevaluating her plan and making tough decisions.

Agility is the ability to adapt and change. Anyssa believes it's hard to learn agility compared to the skills needed in making thorough plans. She believes adaptability is about being comfortable with ambiguity and working in gray areas. This mindset has helped her in her ELG program manager role.

Because ELG is a young company, it has not had the longevity to solve problems and put processes in place. Every day we're addressing situations we've never experienced before. We should have the mindset for working in gray areas, and we need to be ready to make decisions, reevaluate our plans, and forge new pathways. The ability to accept change and make quick decisions is essential. It takes time. *Trust your abilities your decision-making skills.*

Activity: Take Action

Learning to pivot is essential to growth. Let's see how well you pivot throughout a week.

Using the tool below, take a moment and draw a picture of how you would describe how you plan to end this week. Example: "By the end of the week, I plan to have finished xyz."

Throughout the day, there are detours and barriers to reaching the planned destination (the picture we drew). Document your daily journey and identify the roadblocks that you encountered.

How many times did you create a solution to an unplanned obstacle?

Did you reach your final destination? If not, why not? And what were your lessons learned?

Learning to pivot is essential to growth.

Let's see how well you pivot throughout a week.

Using the tool below. Take a moment and draw a picture of how you would describe how you plan to end this week.

By the end of the week, I plan to have finished xyz.

_____

_____

_____

Throughout the day, there are detours and barriers to reaching the planned destination (the picture we drew). Document your daily journey and identify roadblocks that you encountered.

_____

_____

_____

_____

_____

How many times did you create a solution to an unplanned obstacle?

_____

_____

Did you reach your final destination?
If not, why not and what were your lessons learned.

_____

_____

Chapter Nine

Stop and Smell the Roses

TOWARD THE END OF THE WIZARD OF OZ,
Dorothy and her friends spot the Emerald City.
Before they can reach it, they come upon a large
field of red poppies. The Witch of the West casts a
spell over the field, and Dorothy, Toto, and the Lion
fall asleep. It seems they are not going to make it to
the city when the Scarecrow and the Tinman begin
screaming for help.

Hearing their cries, Glenda casts a spell to make
it snow, and everyone wakes up. Just as the group is
about to celebrate their triumph, they discover that
the snow had rusted the Tinman. They add oil to
him and get him moving again. Ever had a day like

that? Once you put out one fire, three more pop up?

What happens next in the story is important. Dorothy and friends don't commiserate over their misfortune. Instead, they begin singing and start dancing and skipping down the yellow brick road once again. All their misfortunes are behind them. They are celebrating their triumphs over adversity and are joyous that they are once again on the road toward their goal of meeting the wizard.

It is hard to remain positive when we are exhausted, frustrated, and angry. None of us live in that 1939 movie where everything is bright and happy and where happy endings are expected. Even so, we can create that joyful and thankful spirit in our lives. We can continue to smile and dance toward our goals.

In Living Color

My grandmother was always there for me, even when I became an adult. I would call often to tell her about my triumphs and tribulations. One time, when I was struggling in my marriage, I called her for advice.

She responded to my dilemma with, "Now, Angie, I want you to listen to me. You need to focus on your marriage a little differently. When we get off the phone, I want you to write ten things you love about your husband." This was a tall order because, at that moment, I was frustrated and angry.

"I can't think of anything positive. I'm too upset," I replied.

"I'll help you out and get you started. Remember, he's a great painter," she offered. Was she serious?

"Painter?"

"Yes, painter. Think about all the times you've changed the colors in your house, and he has always done a great job of painting the walls for you."

She was right. I wasn't seeing what was right in front of me and paying gratitude toward it. There was significance in someone seeing your vision and helping you create it in reality. He knew I changed colors as my moods changed, and as my vision of my home shifted.

In *The Wizard of Oz,* there is that moment when Dorothy lands in Oz and opens the door to a technicolor world. Up to that point, the movie was all in black and white. Seeing those colors, bright and vibrant, helped shift the mood of the audience. It created a new world full of possibilities, wonder, and beauty. I have vibrant color on my walls in my home and in my office. Color energizes me and allows my creativity to flow, so my grandmother's response regarding my husband's painting skills is something, 22 years later, I would have to agree with. Having a partner who understands how color impacts my psyche is critical.

My husband was supporting me and providing me the labor to make those changes. I was missing what was in front of me because I was frustrated and angry at the time. Once I could slow down and take a breath, I could see all the things I appreciated about my husband. Oh, I was still irritated, but it helped me have more perspective on our relationship. And all of a sudden, I could add nine more things to the list with a little more ease. The wisdom of my grandmother was unmatched.

Take a Breath

Ah...the joy of success! You deserve to take some time to enjoy what you've created so far. It is your baby. Marvel at how it has grown!

We are so busy in our lives that we can forget to breathe and just be in the moment. Small and large accomplishments should be celebrated. Celebrations can vitalize us, heal us, motivate us, and lift us up. Taking time and taking stock of where we are, who is around us, and how far we have come helps us to be thankful and brings gratitude into our lives.

My children are all about what's Next. They are ready to move on to the next thing and don't take time to appreciate what they've accomplished. We go through a day, we've accomplished everything we set out to do, and the immediate question I receive is, "What are we doing tomorrow?"

My thought is, "Can we just breathe? Can we just take a moment and appreciate what we've done *today*?"

If we miss moments of gratitude in our lives, we can become frustrated and slip off track from our vision. This not only can impact us directly, but it can also affect friends, colleagues, and even family members. Our day to day struggles can overwhelm us, if we let them. Take time and smell the roses. Remember why you decided to begin the journey toward your vision and appreciate those who have helped you along the way.

The Date

As I mentioned earlier, my husband helped me in the early days of ARDX with operations. He was not happy in that position, but he did it because he believed in my vision. It isn't easy working in the same company as your spouse. The goal is to keep things compartmentalized and not allow work life to invade home life, and vice versa. This can be exceedingly difficult, and when something happens at home and emotions flare, it can drag emotions into the workplace. The opposite often occurs as well.

To keep our relationship in check and to appreciate one another, we created a game for our date nights. Over the course of the date, we would share ten things we loved and enjoyed about one another. This game helped to shift the mood and focus, bringing us back into a space of appreciation, gratitude, and love. Just as Grandma taught me many years ago.

The Renewal

When our 25th wedding anniversary came around, my husband and I wanted to celebrate in a meaningful way. We wanted to commemorate that we had made it, even when the road was pretty bumpy at times. For so many years we'd had each other's backs and got through challenging times together.

So many things had transpired in our lives: three children, four business ventures, four homes, moves to three different cities, a recession, deaths in our family. For moments I felt like I was back in that cocoon, and it was hard to breathe.

The fact that 25 years later we could look at each other and still laugh together is everything. Always enjoying each other's company was worth a celebration. We journeyed, and we made it!

For that special day, we chose 50 people who were champions in our lives to share that moment with. Some of them had been with us since our first date, others at our wedding, while others we met along the way. All of them had been there for us during our ups and downs.

Our three children walked me down the aisle and together we jumped the broom. This was a nod to our original wedding where the two of us jumped the broom. Now our family consisted of the five of us, and we built our home and our life together.

At the ceremony, we renewed our vows, and our pastor asked the community, our 50 guests, to vow to lift us up when we are down. To believe in our unity and support us through the next 25 years.

There were beautiful round boxes full of live butterflies given to the guests, who then opened and released them back into the world. They flew higher and higher as the musicians played a jazzy rendition of Michael Jackson's "You Give Me

Butterflies." At that moment those butterflies represented endurance, hope, change, and life.

This was a renewal of our vows as a couple, as a family, and as a community. This was special.

Milestones

Statistics say that 80% of new businesses fail their first year, and of those that see year two, 50% fail by year five. Within 90 days of starting the company, I quickly realized that these statistics were real. Daily, there are decisions that entrepreneurs make that could lead them down a dark path that makes it difficult, if not impossible, to keep their lights on. From becoming disconnected from the market, to selecting the wrong team, negative cashflow, to creating unattractive pricing models, it is enough to make your head spin.

Each year that our door remained open was a major milestone. We were beating the odds, and that deserved a celebration. What I came to realize is that employees don't join an organization understanding how they are actors in this script that will tell the story of a successful business, or in some cases, an unsuccessful business. They are simply thinking about the job they were hired to do. I recognized that I needed to bring them along for the ride and explain the story to them, and our annual anniversary celebrations allowed me to do just that.

These celebrations were not just for the employees, but it was also important for them to bring someone who was a champion in their lives. Why? I know that the people who hear about your good days and your bad days are more supportive when they too understand the story. When we vent to those close to us, they can only help us think things through when they have an understanding of the spirit of the organization. In other words, they talk us off the ledge when we are making rash and emotion-driven decisions.

Our first anniversary, we had less than a handful of associates, and so we enjoyed an intimate dinner at one of the finest steakhouses in the area. I remember that first one vividly as that was the only celebration that my grandmother was alive to witness. Each year the celebrations grew in size and the themes changed. On our 5th anniversary we celebrated with a live band and the theme was the Roaring 20s. Our 10th year, we celebrated at the opera house with the premier of the ARDX movie.

While the numbers grew, the faces changed and the themes were different, but what remained the same was this intimate time with those who were actors in this performance called ARDX. This was my time to shine the light on them and share the ARDX story. I cherished these moments because they motivated me to continue. Even when my heart was broken, I kept pushing. Even when I was disappointed, I kept pushing. Even when there were long days and nights and not a soul said, "thank you," I kept pushing.

As I took the stage at the 10th year anniversary and looked out into the audience of my associates, leaders, board of advisors, friends, family, and community partners, I stood and inhaled. I allowed my lungs to take it all in. I took in the sweet aroma of the roses from the garden I had planted 10 years ago. The garden that I tended, day in and day out. At that moment, I realized that I was creating history—a legacy. We had beaten the odds.

After I exhaled, the first words out of my mouth were, "Thank you. Thank you to my Lord and Savior for the strength to push through. Thank you to my associates who contributed to our success. Thank you to my incredible family for their many sacrifices." I never saw year ten in my mind. I simply just put one foot in front of the other and followed the yellow brick road.

Annual Awards

During the celebrations, we acknowledged our top performers. It was important to have as much pomp and circumstance as the Academy Awards. After all, the founder may be the lead actor, but there are not many award-winning one-woman shows. And even in those cases, there were those working behind the camera who assisted with the success of that blockbuster performance.

Each year we acknowledge two individuals, our Star Performer and our Employee of the Year. The Employee of the Year award was named in honor of my Grandmother, Olivia Maggie Dyson. This award was given to an individual who embodied the core values of ARDX and made the impossible possible, just as my grandmother did. Each time I announced this award and told the story, it was extremely personal for me, and I felt that she was with me at each of these annual celebrations.

What was beautiful about those moments was that when the names were announced, there was the rousing applause from the audience. We created the type of magic in the organization that meant the whole team was happy for the success of another team member. Yes, I am sure that the awardees appreciated the beautiful trophy and the financial reward, but I am sure they will always remember the experience of their name being called by the CEO and their peers giving them a standing ovation. It is at those times that I think about Maya Angelou's words: "People will forget what you said; and people will forget the things that you do, but people will never forget the way you made them feel."

I believe, years later, those moments of shining the light of gratitude on those who made an impact is a feeling they will always remember.

The Pitch

The weeklong ELG camp for girls is intense. There are a lot of emotions and a lot of hard work that happens. For many of the girls, it's a week of firsts. First time leaving and being away from home. First time traveling. First time thinking of themselves as entrepreneurs. It's their first time coming up with the concept of business. And their first time talking and presenting to a group of people.

The last day of camp is the day they present their Passion Pitch. After this, they can return home and use their Passion Pitch to sell their idea to others with the confidence that they can take their company—and community—to the next level. The

Passion Pitch is the culmination of hard work and overcoming self-doubt.

When those girls (the average age is 10 years old) walk into the classroom and there are three adults who are business leaders, they are indeed giants in the minds of these girls. The girls project their slide deck and speak with conviction about their business concept. Each time I see this, I still get chills. To think that just five days earlier they would barely say their names loud enough to understand them. Each time they exit the room, I give them a high-five and they give me the biggest hug. They did it! They scaled the tallest mountain and they were victorious.

Parents and community leaders join us for the closing ceremony, and we announce the top three pitches. On the spot, the top three pitches are presented on stage in front of over 200 people. They are simply amazing. We then give the $500 award to the top pitch. The girls are so excited for the winner, and it is confirmation to me that this program transforms girls and builds confidence. I know adults who could never speak on the spot, without notes, to an audience of 200 people.

These girls leave understanding the power of their voices. We celebrate their success!

Celebrating the Small Moments

Author and inspirational speaker Simon Sinek authored a book called *Start with Why*. He postulated that even if successful people like Steve Jobs and Martin Luther King Jr. may come from different walks of life, they both started their legacies with a "why." They realized that others would not join in their vision or buy their product unless they understood the "why" behind it.

Annually, we tell our "why" at our ELG Young Girls Rule event. During this event we have a captive audience of 500 to 600 people to explain our ELG why. Simply put, we share the data that proves that we are transforming communities of poverty into communities of power through the power and promise of middle school girls. After just one year in the program, our girl bosses are officially "thousandaires." Before they are even teenagers, they have earned at least $1,000 selling goods and services born out of their passion.

Bigger than the dollars, we are demonstrating to the guest that if each of us uses our skills and is willing to serve our community, we can make a difference. It all starts by understanding our "why."

When our girls and their parents tell their story, it is clear that our ELG Why has ripple effects. The girls are more confident and determined to succeed, their siblings are inspired to be the best they can be, their parents create bigger dreams for themselves, their friends are learning through the girls' words and actions, and communities are being transformed.

Case Study: Aralyn and Heidi

People ask me why I invest so much time and money into ELG, these girls, and their families. Unless you've given selflessly, it's hard for people to understand why. My life is about being of service to my family, my business partners, my friends, and my community. The amount of love and gratitude I receive in return makes my investment seem small and paltry. What I receive in return feeds my soul and energizes my ambitions to do more.

Let me tell you about Aralyn. She was a shy 12-year-old girl when she started at ELG. Her mother, Heidi, wanted to provide something for her daughter that would allow her to tap into her creative soul. ELG seemed to be the right fit for Aralyn.

Heidi had to take a leap of faith. She had never allowed her daughter to spend the night with anyone other than her grandmother. If she wanted her daughter to participate in ELG, she would need to let her go away to be under the care of strangers.

While at ELG camp, Heidi remarked she didn't have time to miss her, and her daughter never got homesick until the last day when she ran out of snacks. Every day, videos, photos, and letters were sent home by the counselors. ELG helped Aralyn to connect with others, and she started her own company, Comics, Inc., which helps children with illiteracy.

When Aralyn returned from camp, she had come out of her shell and was more confident. She started making more friends in school and became more focused on her future as a Girl Boss.

Her mother works hard and is raising other children. She couldn't have provided all the resources and trips and programs for her daughter. Heidi has said many times how grateful she is for the opportunities that ELG has provided for Aralyn.

To see these young girls grow into young entrepreneurs is my "why." I collect and remember all of these stories and think about how much good we've done. It inspires me to want to do even more for girls like Aralyn in the future.

Activities: Take Action

Take time each day, or at least each week, to really appreciate what you've built. We are often so busy and lost in the details of our work that we don't truly value what we've done. You may have hundreds of employees, but how do you make their lives better? You may be solving critical issues for your clients, but how are you making an impact? You may be providing a resource that saves a life. How does that feel? Enjoy what you've cultivated...you deserve it!

Chapter Ten

Congruence

WE STARTED our ELG journey in seven states. It grew to nine, then 30, and now the movement has spread to 48 states. The year 2020 was as far as the vision had been planted in me back in 2017. After all, 2020 seemed so far away then. Reaching 1,000 girls in 48 states seemed like an audacious goal back when we were still trying to build our stakeholder group in our initial seven states.

As we continued our journey in the spring of 2019 and were making plans to touch 600 girls in 30 states, I remember calling out in prayer, what is the vision beyond 2020? What would our next step be?

It was not even a week later when I received an email from a current Ph.D. student at OSU. She had been following my study and came out to hear my presentation at the Academy of Management Conference back in 2018. She was interested in building on my research and asked if I would be willing to bring the study to her home of Nigeria.

We began corresponding and eventually she came to observe the program in the summer of 2019, when she confirmed that she was interested in opening doors for ELG in Nigeria.

This was only the beginning to my prayers being answered. One month after our final summer session in 2019, I received a call from one of our newly appointed Board of Advisor members. She was Haitian-American and spoke with such conviction about ELG going to Haiti. Within a few months we were in conversations with private school owners in Haiti and the negotiations began.

ELG 2.0 was born and God granted my request. ELG goes global in the Summer of 2020, with girl bosses in Nigeria and Haiti. I don't believe for a moment that is the end of the ELG story—and we are ready to expand further as the need presents itself.

Not only are we growing our geographical reach, but we're also developing our program. ELG 2.0 now provides college prep and funding to help these girl bosses enter into and graduate from college. We realized that mentoring and support should not stop in high school. We will continue to go deeper with the 1,000 girl bosses in the U.S. while growing our footprint abroad. I was reminded of the Prayer of Jabez:

Jabez cried out to the God of Israel, "Oh, that you would bless me and enlarge my territory! Let your hand be with me, and keep me from harm so that I will be free from pain." And God granted his request. 1 Chronicles 14:10

So much of the ELG story has been an answer to a prayer and things have simply fallen in place. Everything has a season and its own special time. It is at these moments that I recognize that I am operating in the space designed for me. All the roads I have travelled in my life have placed me just where I am at this moment. Perfectly positioned to reach out and grab the opportunities that have come my way to live out the vision for my life. Just as in the prayer of Jabez, ELG has come without pain. I know that it has been guided by the author of my book of life and I am finally living in complete congruence with my life.

Balancing the Seesaw

Congruence: [kən'gro¯oəns] NOUN   agreement or harmony; compatibility.

I often hear friends and associates speaking of their quest for work/life balance. The common questions I am asked when I speak to groups of women are: How do you do it all? How do you achieve work/life balance? I really had to think hard about this question. These questions are important, and it seems to be universal in the women from all over who are asking.

As I began to reflect on my answers, I came to the conclusion that the work/life balance idea is a myth. There is no scale that will say, you are now giving equal amounts of yourself mentally and emotionally to your "work" and your "home". As I reflect on my life, there were seasons (days, weeks, months, and years) that I have sacrificed one for the other. I have given myself permission to accept that the sacrifice would pay off in the long run.

The balance is not a static log on the ground, in perfect balance and unmoving. The work/life balance is a seesaw. When one part goes up in priority, the other goes down, and then we shift the opposite way. Up and down—not balanced in the sense that our lives sit in perfect peace and perfection.

What happens when that seesaw only stays in one way—when our priorities keep it up in one direction? We might be sitting low in our relationships and our purpose, but high in our time at work and staying busy. What happens then?

I find so many people who are in careers that don't feed their souls. It puts food on the table, but it doesn't feed their souls. They sacrifice a piece of themselves to have a high income, but they are sitting low in every other aspect of their lives. They give up so much every day in their 9-5 hours, they feel like something is being taken from them. I also speak with many entrepreneurs who spend time floating from one "networking" event to another without a real value proposition. Or some who call themselves serial entrepreneurs, starting multiple organizations before they have a thriving single organization. They want to keep the work up high and fail to see that the more weight they are adding, the harder it is to shift the seesaw back the other way.

My secret to accomplishing the goals thus far and having a feeling of peace is operating in congruence. All parts of my life must work in harmony. Up and down the seesaw goes, sometimes slow, sometimes fast. My key has been touching something once and accomplishing five things. Then shifting to something else.

Family is a major component of my life, so it is important that they are factored into my equation. My eldest daughter is the program manager of ELG; my youngest daughter is in the ELG program. My son records our sessions. This means, when I am away running the summer program, I am not away from my children because they are actively engaged in the program. The congruence allows a smoother transition because sometimes work is play, and play becomes a part of work. In these cases, the plank I am going up and down on becomes straight, and I have the two sides of my life working together. This is as close to the idea of work/life balance that I have found.

ELG has become an important priority for the entire Reddix family, so much so that my 15-year-old son will email ideas regarding the next year's camp and how the video production can be smoother.

This has also given us an unexpected gift. During one of our home church experiences, our question was regarding the gifts we receive from each other. My youngest daughter expressed how much pride she feels seeing her mother in action during the ELG program. She said hearing my teachings as a participant in the ELG program has helped her understand the lessons she received from me at home. This is what harmony looks like!

I am selective about the speaking engagements that I accept. They must be in congruence with the goals that I have established for my life. If I am speaking, it must be in a setting where I will learn from the audience something that will make my presentation stronger and put me in circles that will move my organizations' missions forward.

After I received my Ph.D., I was asked to adjunct at Norfolk State University School of Business, a local HBCU. I was honored to have been asked but understood clearly what I had on my plate already. My request was that I teach a topic that represents that world I live in, entrepreneurship. The information I use in that program is the information I share in my manager's training at ARDX. It is the information I share with the advanced cohorts of Envision Lead Grow. I am continuing to build in the area that is congruent with other aspects of my life.

As we grow older, and hopefully a little wiser, we're given the gift of perspective. This isn't something you can learn in a classroom or a textbook; it comes from life experience. If I had the chance to talk to my 10-year-old self, I would say that while you may struggle and the path isn't always entirely clear, there IS a purpose in your life—just follow the yellow brick road. And remember that you are perfectly and wonderfully creative.

If I had the chance to talk to my 25-year-old self, I would say, "Relax!" While it's true that all my hard work has helped me create the security I now have, I missed many opportunities to spend time with my friends and family. Never forget what is important in life and who sustains you.

What would you say to your younger self?

How do you manage all the parts of your life and still take time out for the people who are important to you?

Building Something New

I run and manage two for-profit companies and two non-profit companies. For them to be successful and for me to be the best wife and mother I can be, everything has to work together. There has to be congruence with everything I do to keep the seesaw moving smoothly and to find the benefit not only for me, but also to those around me: my family, friends, associates, board members, and my community.

This means that I have been very selective about starting my new businesses. They have to fit (be congruent) with what I have already created. These new ventures were natural extensions of my mothership, ARDX. The central goal was to help provide services that promote healthy minds, healthy bodies, and even healthy economies. My new businesses had to make sense in the context of the rest of my life.

I'm not building tires in one place and running a daycare in another. Everyone, in all aspects of my life, is in alignment. I started the new companies when it was the right time, too. When there was a demand for something new, and when it aligned with all the other aspects of my business and my life, then of course I needed to create it.

People try to emulate what they see before they understand it. People ask me how I was able to start new businesses. I am always cautious about answering because I don't want to give the impression this is something that I recommend people do. First, you must have a solid company (your foundation). It does not make sense to try to start something new if your first company is in its infancy. I encourage people to focus their time in resources in their first venture before even beginning to think about another one.

When I began my dissertation, it was never my intention to use it to begin a company. It was to focus on what was important to me. I wanted to help young girls who were like me see a different perspective of their future, grab onto their strength, and emerge as boss women.

The turning point (the demand) occurred once I realized that I wanted to continue to work with these girls. I was donating my time and money into the project, and so I was already committed, but I knew I could not continue on my own. That is when I decided to create a new organization so that we could serve more girls in more communities and have the resources set up to do it. The demand was there, and it was congruent with my company and my personal goals.

That is why having the right people around you, supporting your vision, is so important. When I wanted to go back to school, I was able to rearrange my schedule so that my business could continue to run smoothly. I had associates who supported me and made sure that could happen. My family was flexible and took care of things when I had to be out of town.

Some of these same people stepped up when I began ELG. They wanted to help me grow my vision. It was not a totally new vision or direction; it was an extension of what I had already created.

I foster relationships that help that alignment. When opportunities arise for me to learn and increase my knowledge, I have to decide whether taking the time to do that activity will benefit *all* aspects of my life. It has to be time well spent and relevant to my vision.

Everything I love exists in my business and my life. It is a balancing act, a seesaw up and down, but I work hard every day to be sure that each business and each project feeds everything else. Some days this is a smooth operation, and others I have to roll up my sleeves and make adjustments. But because I strive to make all aspects of my life congruent, it is easier to grow where I have been planted, and where I can also plant new seeds when the opportunities arise.

The Meaning of Envision Lead Grow

When we have a life that is congruent, we can create something beautiful. I was the black butterfly soaring to new heights in my life and my career in ARDX, and then I was presented with the new idea of adding ELG in my life, and into the lives of my family and those whom I worked with. Butterflies pollinate flowers as they move in their lives. This pollination promotes new life so that things can grow and produce new flowers and plants.

ELG was a new flower, but I needed it to be congruent with the company and vision I had already established. I remember sharing my thoughts with a dear friend, and together we created a name that had meaning far beyond the three simple words.

Envision: I always say we must start with the end in mind. I strongly believe there are no limits when we can actually see ourselves being who we intend to be. Visualization is powerful. This wis congruent not only with the first seed, but it also underpins everything in my life. It all begins with a vision.

Lead: I don't believe people can "knight" us to be the leader of our future. Leadership begins within each of us. We can't wait for others to provide step-by-step instruction, but we must take initiative and lead ourselves down the yellow brick road. We may fall along the way, but that is still progress. Within ARDX, others called me "boss." At first this was irritating, but what they were saying was that they respected me as a leader. I could not designate myself a leader; I had to act as a leader. My purpose in ELG is to release the boss girls within every girl we work with, so that they can learn to be the leaders of tomorrow.

Grow: We must grow where we are planted. We are in a specific place for a reason and we must make the most of any situation with a strong determination to learn from the existing experience, bad or good. I believe it is all for our good to learn, learn, and continue to learn. It is sometimes hard to see our purpose or make sense of things that happen in our lives. When we realize that everything in our lives has a purpose, and that we can learn from our challenges, we have the opportunity to grow with no bounds.

The Legacy

New things were beginning to grow around me. My new businesses were having an impact well beyond the confines of their original purpose. They were growing a legacy. Although butterflies soar high and are beautiful for those who behold them, they don't live very long. But their short lives have a huge impact on the lives of all living creatures.

As we stop to drink the nectar from flowers, we're also cross-pollinating our message, our knowledge, and our essence to others in our lives. For me, my pollination has been and will continue to be in the lives of young women. They need care and direction to find their way, so that they can become the most beautiful, strong, and successful women that the world has yet to know. I can help guide and nurture them.

Everything I have built and have yet to build are with the purpose of growth beyond my time—my legacy. I'm leaving behind the chance for new caterpillars to go through the cycle to take my place and soar even higher than I have in my lifetime. My commitment is not only to leave the world in better shape than when I entered it, but I also want to leave a legacy that makes it even better after my time on earth comes to an end.

SMART Girls

In ELG we are not just building boss girls who will take the world over with their new, innovative and brilliant businesses, we are also building SMART girls. We are building girls who will become the CEOs of their lives and learn how to live with purpose, mindfulness, and with congruence.

This is a part of the legacy I want to leave to each of these girls. Like the eight seeds, I want to plant a mindset within them that will help them become the butterflies I can already see within each of them—because each of them was me.

What does SMART mean?

Strong. We are strong in who we are. We are capable.

Mistakes. Perfection is not the goal; rather, we learn from our mistakes.

Applaud. We applaud our sisters and lift them up.

Rise. We rise because we are resilient. That gives us the power to move forward.

Total Package. We are the total package. We are unique, wonderful, and allowed to be who we are.

Whether you are a girl who is reading this, or a mother, a teacher, a mentor or a counselor, I hope I have provided you something, some little nugget that you can take away and us to build a better life not only for you, but also for everyone you touch in your lives. Thank you for taking this journey with me! Let's soar high together!

Black Butterfly
Set the skies on fire
Rise up even higher
So the ageless winds of time can catch your wings...

Activity: Take Action

In my talks, I often ask the participants to write a letter to themselves as a self-commitment. I collect their notes, and in six months, the messages they wrote are mailed back to them. They can see what they promised themselves and determine how well they are doing.

What is the promise you will make to yourself? When you are done, seal the envelope and write on it "Open on..." Write a date six months in the future.

"You have plenty of courage, I'm sure," answered Oz. "All you need is confidence in yourself. There is no living thing that isn't afraid when it faces danger. The true courage is in facing danger when you are afraid, and that kind of courage you have in plenty."

– L. Frank Baum, *The Wonderful Wizard of Oz*

Bibliography

Baum, L Frank, *The Wonderful Wizard of Oz* New York: New York. Harper Collins, 2000.

Chmielewski, Dawn, "More mainstream movies for Netflix online". *Los Angeles Times.* October 1, 2008.

Covey, Stephen. *The 7 Habits of Highly Effective People: Powerful Lessons in Personal Change.* New York: New York. Simon and Schuster. (2013)

Ericsson, K A, Krampe, R T Tesch-Romer, C., "The role of deliberate practice in the acquisition of expert performance" *Psychological Review*, volume 100, issue 3, p. 363 – 406 (1993)

King, Martin L. "I Have a Dream." Speech presented at the March on Washington for Jobs and Freedom, Washington, D.C., August 1968.
http://avalon.law.yale.edu/20th_century/mlk01.asp.

Madsen, Dag Øivind, "SWOT Analysis: A Management Fashion Perspective", *International Journal of Business Research* **16**:1:39-56 (2016)

Mattone, John, *The Intelligent Leader: Unlocking the 7 Secrets to Leading Others and Leaving Your Legacy.* New York: New York. Wiley. (2019) P. 29.

Pedley, Richard. *Crafting a Vision.* Regenprenuer.com. Retrieved 03-16-2020.
https://www.regenpreneur.com/crafting-a-vision.html

Project Management Institute. (2004). *A guide to the project management body of knowledge (PMBOK guide).* Newtown Square, Pa: Project Management Institute

Reddix, A. D. (2017). Super Girl Power: Can Girls Move Swiftly Through Deliberate Practice to Become Successful Entrepreneurs?

Rhimes, Shonda, *Year of Yes: How to Dance It Out, Stand In the Sun and Be Your Own Person.* New York: New York. Simon and Schuster. (2016)

Robert A. Baron, Robert A, Henry, Rebecca A. "How entrepreneurs acquire the capacity to excel: insights from research on expert performance." *Strategic Entrepreneurship Journal,* 2010; 4 (1): 49 DOI: 10.1002/sej.82

Rubin, Robert S., "Will the Real SMART Goals Please Stand Up?" *The Industrial-Organizational Psychologist.* April, Volume 39. Number 4. P.26-27. (2002)

Schawbel, Dan, "Denise Morrison: How She Became The First Woman CEO at Campbell Soup Company." Forbes.com. Retrieved March 16, 2020.
https://www.forbes.com/sites/danschawbel/2017/11/06/denise-morrison-how-she-became-the-first-woman-ceo-at-campbell-soup-company/#284b4ee46be4

Stemmie, Karen and Stemmie, Dennis, *The Power of Setbacks: How to Turn Your Mess Into Your Success at Any Age.* P. 19. New York: New York. Morgan James. (2017)

Williams, Deniece, "Black Butterfly." *Let's Hear it for the Boy.* Mann, Barry and Well, Cynthia. Columbia Records. (1984)

Winfrey, Oprah. "Every Person Has a Purpose." Oprah.com, Retrieved March 16, 2020.
https://www.oprah.com/spirit/how-oprah-winfrey-found-her-purpose.

About ELG

In the United States there are 39.7 million people living in poverty; women and children make up 70% percent of the impoverished. More than 1 in 3 single mother families live in poverty and that number increases amongst people of color. With the rise of the number of little girls living in poverty and an increase in outside influences warping their self-image and self-worth bringing about life and death burdens caused by social media and other peer pressures, we must build a society that empowers them. Therefore, changing the mindsets of the little girls in those populations can transform a community from poverty to prosperity.

We must build the confidence of little girls ages 10-14, to hear their own voices. Using the 'Deliberate Practice' theory, we can connect girls to their possibilities and thus tap into their power. The 'Deliberate Practice' theory states that 10,000 hours of purposeful and systematic practice applied in a focused fashion, creates an expert. My program, Envision Lead Grow, applies this theory to educate, train, and develop young entrepreneurs around the country. Let us create a new generation of expert businesswomen to eliminate poverty, misogyny, and race-based discrimination by giving the power to tomorrow's boardrooms.

I was a little girl born into poverty. But I was fortunate enough to have a mother who showed me my power and promise. She taught me the importance of earning, saving a dollar, and how to make money multiply for our family and me. Today as an entrepreneur who employs more than 100 people, I have the great opportunity to employ others in the community and empowering their families to prosper for generations to come. I believe that the model of my success can be replicated throughout the United States by teaching, training, and developing impressionable girls.

By 2020, Envision Lead Grow will have 1,000 little girls, ages 10 – 18, in the pipeline to become business owners. Using that foundation, if each one of them employs 100 people that will result in 100,000 people with jobs in our nation.

For more information please check out our website:

https://envisionleadgrow.org/

About Author

Dr. Angela D. Reddix is a visionary and innovative thinker with global perspective and entrepreneurial drive. As a passionate mentor and advisor to the next generation of young girls and women, Angela is a leading advocate for entrepreneurship as a way of creating positive transformation in the world. Her own entrepreneurial drive led Angela to found ARDX, an award-winning healthcare management and IT consulting firm dedicated to improving the lives of our nation's most vulnerable populations.

She also serves as Founder and Chairman of Envision Lead Grow, a Norfolk-based nonprofit organization aimed at aspiring girls of all ages to chart their destinies by teaching them the critical skills and dedication it takes to accomplish their dreams through entrepreneurship; which inspired her 2020 TEDx talk.

Dr. Reddix's, unique ability to inspire greatness through the lessons of her own story has earned her a coveted position on the Old Dominion University's Entrepreneurial Hall of Fame, the Humanitarian Award presented by the Virginia Center for Inclusive Communities, the Women of Achievement Award presented by Old Dominion University, ODU's Entrepreneur of the Year and Founder's Day Regional Service Awards, the Leading Ladies of Hampton Roads Award presented by Coastal Virginia Business Magazine, the US Chamber of Commerce's Big Blue-Ribbon Award, Inside Business's Women in Business Award, and many other notable achievements.

Committed to lifelong learning and achievement, Dr. Angela currently teaches Entrepreneurship and Business at Norfolk State University. She received her bachelor's degree in Business Administration in Marketing from James Madison University, a master's degree in Organizational Development from Bowie State University with a focus on Training, a graduate certificate in Healthcare Compliance from The George Washington University, and her Ph.D. in Business Administration from Oklahoma State University. Dr. Angela resides in Virginia Beach, Virginia and has a husband and three children.

Index

CPSIA information can be obtained
at www.ICGtesting.com
Printed in the USA
LVHW020934310520
656912LV00005B/490